Sacagawea's Nickname

Essays on the American West

Sacagawea's Nickname

Essays on the American West

Larry McMurtry

NEW YORK REVIEW BOOKS

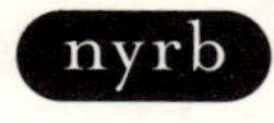

New York

THIS IS A NEW YORK REVIEW BOOK

PUBLISHED BY THE NEW YORK REVIEW OF BOOKS

SACAGAWEA'S NICKNAME
ESSAYS ON THE AMERICAN WEST

by Larry McMurtry

This edition published in 2001
in the United States of America by
The New York Review of Books
1755 Broadway
New York, NY 10019
www.nybooks.com

Library of Congress Cataloging-in-Publication Data

McMurtry, Larry.
Sacagawea's nickname : essays on the American West / by Larry McMurtry.
p. cm.
ISBN 0-940322-92-7 (hardcover : alk. paper)
1. West (U.S.) — History. 2. West (U.S.) — Biography. 3. West (U.S.) — Historiography. 4. Frontier and pioneer life — West (U.S.) 5. Indians of North America — West (U.S.) — History. I. Title.
F591 .M388 2001
978'.02 — dc21

2001004674

ISBN 0-940322-92-7

Printed in the United States of America on acid-free paper.

November 2001

For Barbara Epstein

Contents

Introduction

In symbolism and popular myth the American West is often treated as one habitat when in fact it's several: mountain, desert, forest, plain. Much of it is too dry, some of it very wet. I can take any amount of dry, but not much wet. In the Pacific Northwest I feel smothered, soaked, and claustrophobic. I'm not fond of the Rocky Mountains, either—they take up entirely too much sky. I can get by, and even flourish, in what one might call the southern Southwest, a strip extending from the Big Bend of the Rio Grande to the very borders of West Hollywood, but I am really a native of the plains, the sea of grass that flows north from the Texas Panhandle way up past Calgary. The plains can boast few hills, few cities, and few trees—they offer, to put it mildly, the kind of country where one can really breathe.

By the time of my birth, in 1936, the part of the south plains where I was raised was already essentially the oil patch, but my own family had no oil and rather scorned it; we belonged, proudly and already a little anachronistically, to the modest small-ranch herding culture: an old culture in world terms, though new enough in Texas.

In my teens, already a failed cowboy, I realized that—one way or another—my work was going to be with words, not herds, though, of course, being a word-herder means that one has not entirely escaped the herding imperative. Didn't I just herd a few drifting strays into this paragraph?

The West, to me, was always a place to look at, and I have looked at most of it many times, becoming, in the process, a kind of connoisseur of western skies, whose space and sweep still move me.

What I never wanted to do, in regard to the West, was read about it. As soon as I got to a place where books were—in my case, Rice University—I began to suck in knowledge about the great world and the old cultures which formed it. Like most ambitious young readers I made an immediate assault on the high moderns—Joyce, Woolf, Lawrence, Proust, Rilke, Kafka, Hemingway, Faulkner, Eliot, Pound—and then worked my way back, in the course of several decades, through the French, English, and Russian novelists toward Cervantes and Homer, only reaching the last named, with any depth of comprehension, sometime around my sixtieth year.

After literature, or along with it, came history. In "September 1, 1939," W. H. Auden has a famous stanza:

Accurate scholarship can
Unearth the whole offence
From Luther until now
That has driven a culture mad,
Find what occurred at Linz...

I doubt that Auden would be surprised to know that scholarship is still attempting to work out just what *did* occur at Linz, where Hitler grew up. Vast book has followed vast book, and yet no one is still quite able to say with precision why that particular culture went mad.

With so much greatness to absorb, and so much history to learn—not to mention music, art, philosophy, etc.—why would a young man want to waste time reading about the country he could see out the window of his pickup?

What was visible from *my* pickup was a place where there had not been time for much to happen, in social or cultural terms, anyway. My grandparents were pioneers; they stopped at a point in the emptiness and made their start. Henry James, in his famous commentary on Hawthorne and his materials, didn't even think New England offered the novelist enough in the way of social density, but, compared to Archer County, New England seemed as old as Ur or Sumer. The moral and social grapes which produce literature could hardly have had time to ferment in a place as recently settled as the West.

Cyril Connolly, in *Enemies of Promise*, claimed that a writer's sole duty was to produce a masterpiece, but Cyril Connolly spoke from within an old, slow-growing culture. To expect literary masterpieces in any profusion from a place as newly formed as the West would be foolish. Before there can be masterpieces there has to be schooling; throughout the nineteenth century and well into the twentieth the struggle for schooling itself played a large role in the careers of intellectually ambitious westerners. Getting educated took determination—in some cases heroic determination: see the essays on the historian Angie Debo and the conservationist John Wesley Powell. Fortunately, with the growth of university systems and subsystems many modestly sized western towns now have colleges. Young readers and writers no longer need to be lonely in the West, as they were in my own boyhood sixty years ago.

From the mid-Fifties to the mid-Eighties I did a great deal of reviewing for newspapers—fiction, mostly—and I pretty soon found that I was avoiding western books. They made me uneasy, and still do, the fiction particularly. Some of it was worthy, of course, but in literature mere worthiness is the quality most rapidly destined for eternal shade. There were, for example, three prolific westerners whose work kept turning up on my desk: Frederick Manfred, Vardis Fisher, and Wright Morris. Early on Manfred spewed out a Wolfeian trilogy, Fisher a Wolfeian tetralogy. Though university men both, Manfred and Fisher saw themselves as literary mountain men; they poured forth books in a furious stream. Wright Morris, writer and photographer, had a more sophisticated talent. His first work of criticism, *The Territory Ahead*, is excellent, and his book of Venetian photographs, *Venice: A Love Story*, is haunting, but most of his fiction flattens out. As, year after year, the books of these men floated in, it seemed to me that they produced ever diminishing returns. The more they wrote the less they counted, a cruel judgment but, I fear, a fair one. The question that hovered in the back of my mind—and hovers still—is whether the failure was one of talent, or of community. In a smarter West, would they have been better writers? My uneasiness with their books may have been an uneasiness about the culture that produced them.

When, with the encouragement of Barbara Epstein, I began to write on western topics for *The New York Review of Books*, I took another look at my western shelves and was reminded of Northrup Frye's famous theory of modes, so important to graduate students of an earlier day. Frye's modes descend from god-stories or myths through romance and realism to irony; it seems to me that, in truncated form, some such progression did happen in the West. The Indians had the god-stories, Lewis and Clark provided the epic, and the romance came in a century and a half of hero-tales, as the memoirs of mountain men, explorers, merchants from the Santa Fe Trail, emigrants on the Oregon Trail, gold rushers, soldiers of fortune, or real soldiers, come to fight the Indians, found their way into print. Some of this literature is ghost-written bombast, but some of it is honest. Finally, toward the end of the nineteenth century, Stephen Crane came west, wrote "The Bride Comes to Yellow Sky," and encouraged a young Nebraskan named Willa Cather, who didn't stay long in the West but whose gift—particularly in the Nebraska-inspired *O Pioneers!* (1913) and *My Ántonia* (1918) —brought to western fiction a distinction it did not long sustain; between Willa Cather's early work and Wallace Stegner's mature work there is not much fiction out of the West that will hold a reader today.

Frye's modes end with irony, from whence there is sometimes a circling back toward myth (*Ulysses*) and, sure enough, two quirky, exceptional, ironic books did arrive out of the West, one a novel, one a history, both concerned with that moment of turning in western history when myth arises out of epic conflict: the defeat and death of George Armstrong Custer and all his men at the battle of the Little Bighorn in June of 1876. The novel is Thomas Berger's *Little Big Man* (1964), and the history is Evan S. Connell Jr.'s *Son of the Morning Star* (1984).

This is not a literary history, which spares me the necessity of writing about my own generation, except to say that we have been rather parsimonious with masterpieces. Quite possibly the generation of Raymond Carver, Leslie Marmon Silko, Richard Ford, Robert Boswell, Louise Erdrich, and others will leave us old-timers eating their dust.

I should mention, though, an old contrarian strain in western letters which accounts for the very best books: the naturalist-memoirists. One of the most contrarian of this restive tribe, the late Edward Abbey, managed to stay mad at me for a decade for calling him a naturalist and suggesting, even, that he was a kind of western Thoreau. No, no, he thundered—his influences were Nietzsche, Kafka, and Knut Hamsun! I said okay, okay, and paid for his catfish dinner. Ed Abbey's protestations not withstanding, there is a long tradition of meditative outdoorsmen, with sharp eyes and well-stocked minds. Lewis and Clark started it, Audubon and John Muir carried it on; in our time Aldo Leopold's *Sand County Almanac*, John Graves's *Goodbye to a River*, Edward Abbey's *Desert Solitaire*, and Barry Lopez's *Arctic Dreams* are notable examples.

In the essays that follow—though I do attempt to acknowledge two remarkable western women, the poet-novelist Janet Lewis (died age ninety-nine) and the historian Angie Debo (died age ninety-eight)—I have not directly concerned myself with literature. Man may have seven ages, but the West has had only three: the age of Heroes (Lewis and Clark), the age of Publicity (Buffalo Bill), and the age of Suburbia, for which the preferred new term is Urban Sprawl. How we got from the first age to the third, and what we destroyed in the process, is a story historians will be worrying for a long time. Myself, I still mainly like to look.

Chapter 1

THE WEST WITHOUT CHILI

It used to be that the best way for a westerner, male or female, to get mentioned in the papers was to shoot up a town. A certain volume of gunplay, even if ineffective, usually brought instant celebrity, as many an entry in *The New Encyclopedia of the American West*[1] attests. Wordplay, on the other hand—particularly serious wordplay—has not been as warmly welcomed. The world public has always wanted to read about the American West, but, from at least the time of Ned Buntline (Edward Z. C. Judson), its overwhelming preference has been to read the colorful if bizarre fictions that the pulp writers of many countries have so voluminously supplied.

Some readers may recall James Thurber's amusing essay "The French Far West," in which he discusses the French westerns he liked to relax with, in one of which a character named Wild Bird Hickok manages to liberate Pittsburgh, which was under heavy siege by *les peaux-rouges*. One of the more illuminating entries in this big reference book is the one headed "western novelists, European," which makes clear that our homegrown pulpers, industrious though they have been (Zane Grey 78 books, Louis L'Amour 120 at last count, Max Brand—real name Frederick Schiller Faust—a life work estimated at 30 million

1. Edited by Howard R. Lamar (Yale University Press, 1998).

words), are slackers compared to the Europeans. The Norwegian Rudolph Muus has written over 500 westerns, the Frenchman George Fronval more than 600; in the nineteenth century Friedrich Gerstäcker rambled through 150, H. B. Möllhausen managed 178, and Karl May produced the immensely popular Winnetou novels, providing the source, in the 1960s, for an amusing series of Euro-westerns starring Lex Barker as May's hero, Old Shatterhand.

The fact that for more than 150 years millions of readers have been willing to refresh themselves by diving eagerly and repeatedly into this Niagara of froth should give any writer or scholar proposing to write something at least nominally truthful about the West a handsome opportunity for reflection. Is a public that will happily subscribe to the sumptuous leatherette edition of the principal works of Louis L'Amour (in 120 volumes) really likely to care about the intricacies of land-use legislation, or the struggle over water rights in the Great Basin, or the Treaty of Guadalupe Hidalgo, or indeed any of the 2,400 subjects this encyclopedia attempts to address?

The answer is no, and it's been no since Lewis and Clark returned in triumph to St. Louis in 1806; and yet a lot of honest scholars and serious writers grit their teeth and soldier on, well aware that lies about the West—lies that are being projected every day in vivid color on a big screen somewhere—have a potency with the public that their modest truths can rarely match.

The first edition of *The Reader's Encyclopedia of the American West* was published by Thomas Y. Crowell in 1977, in a smaller, considerably less stately format. Before the 1970s Western Studies—if that's an appropriate term—had been a kind of ragbag discipline, perhaps not a discipline at all. A number of good, quirky books got written, but, on the whole, the field had a weedy look. Country editors, prairie schoolmarms, county historians, retired lawyers, lone professors here and there, and not a few raving eccentrics saved a good many records and did a certain amount of useful groundwork. There were heroes among them, not all of whom get due mention in this book. George E. Hyde of Omaha, totally deaf and almost blind, working only with the resources of the Omaha Public Library and what it could get him, wrote his three excellent books about the Sioux,[2] saving segments of tribal history that the Sioux themselves would have lost. *Beyond the Hundredth Meridian*, Wallace Stegner's splendid book on John Wesley Powell, appeared at a time (1954) when not one citizen in ten thousand would have recognized Powell's name, though when he emerged from his pioneering exploration of the Grand Canyon of the Colorado in 1869 he was for a time something of a folk hero and later became an intellectual hero too, because he saw clearly that successful westward expansion into the arid lands would depend on careful management of limited water resources. Walter Prescott Webb published his pioneering study *The Great Plains* in 1931, when no one but himself would have supposed there was anything worth studying about a lot of flat empty grassland. And a Montana newspaperwoman named Helena Huntington Smith managed to corner the old cowboy Teddy Blue Abbott and help him produce the best of all cowboy autobiographies, *We Pointed Them North* (1939).

What was lacking until the 1970s in regard to the American West was something like what the Annales school achieved in France: the kind of critical mass that results when a number of trained intellects are working in full awareness of one another, though of course not in total agreement.

By the 1970s the American studies program at Yale and a number of similar programs elsewhere had begun to produce nestfuls of doctoral candidates, all hungry for subjects—and there stretched the West, as inviting to scholarship as it had once been to other, more arduous forms of exploration. In 1967, a decade before the first edition of this encyclopedia appeared, the Yale-trained historian William H.

2. *Red Cloud's Folk* (1937), *A Sioux Chronicle* (1956), *Spotted Tail's Folk* (1961).

Goetzmann won the history Pulitzer for his impressive book *Exploration and Empire*; from then on the West could be seen to have a certain shine in academic circles. By the mid-1970s, a century after the great sky-darkening swarms of grasshoppers flew down and ate up Kansas, another hungry swarm appeared from the general direction of New Haven, this one composed of would-be Ph.D.'s, as eager to strip the West of thesis topics as the grasshoppers had been to strip it of grain.

This surge of scholarly interest was anticipated at the popular level by Time-Life, which quickly rolled out a twenty-volume series called *The Old West*, each volume being devoted to a given trade (Rivermen, Cowboys, Trail-blazers, Chiefs, Gunfighters, even Canadians!). This series is crammed with pictures, as one might expect, accompanied by texts that vary from not bad to bad; I confess that the majesty of the whole enterprise was diminished for me by the fact that, on the shelf, the set looks a lot like the aforementioned principal works of Louis L'Amour.

By the 1980s the revisionist historians were in full cry, challenging —usually sensibly and often passionately—the long-prevailing triumphalist view of the winning of the West, which was that winning it was a mighty good thing; a dirty job, of course, in some respects, but one that had to be done if we were to fulfill our commitment to Manifest Destiny. On the contrary, cried Patricia Nelson Limerick, Clyde A. Milner II, Charles Rankin, Donald Worster, and a score or so of their colleagues and sympathizers: it was a job, they argued, that had devastated the environment, ruined much of the land, destroyed the native peoples, penalized minorities, wreaked fiscal havoc, and, last but not least, did in tens of thousands of the would-be winners themselves, many of whom won nothing but narrow graves, often within only a hundred miles or so of where the Gateway Arch now stands.

The editor of *The New Encyclopedia*, Howard R. Lamar, well aware that the long, hot debate between revisionists and triumphalists has left a number of sensibilities rather severely scorched, has established something like an equal-time policy for this new edition. If an entry states a revisionist position the contributor is obliged to at least sketch in the position that he or she is in disagreement with.

This is certainly courtly of Professor Lamar, but I'm not sure who he thinks he's fooling. A glance at the contributor's list—fifty contributors are either from or at Yale—makes it clear that revisionists are solidly in command, and since scholars with revisionist leanings have been pouring out of the graduate schools for twenty-five years it would be odd if it were otherwise. The major histories and reference books to appear in the Nineties, including this one, are rife with revisionist overlappings. Richard White, who himself wrote the whole of *'It's Your Misfortune and None of My Own': A New History of the American West* (1993), contributes to *The New Encyclopedia* and to the recent *Oxford History of the American West* (1994) as well. Two of the editors of the *Oxford History*, Clyde A. Milner II and Martha A. Sandweiss, also contribute to *The New Encyclopedia*, several of whose contributors are to be found in the Oxford book—all of which probably only goes to show that the rich get richer. The only recent work of reference not clearly in the revisionist camp is Dan L. Thrapp's three-volume *Encyclopedia of Frontier Biography* (1989), which could have benefited from a little more revisionist vigor.

Despite its editor's polite ground rules *The New Encyclopedia* doesn't entirely avoid revisionist overkill. Why, for example, must the poor old Turner (or Frontier) Thesis, long since battered to its knees, be further pummeled by entries demonstrating that it doesn't hold for Australia or Canada either? Its author, the historian Frederick Jackson Turner, argued, at the end of the last century, that our institutions, our social systems, and perhaps our character had been shaped by an open frontier and the availability of an abundance of land, either cheap or free. Perhaps when these entries were first published, in the 1977 edition, it was not yet evident that the Frontier Thesis was down for the count, so Canada and Australia got piled on, just in case.

As in any big reference book, odd facts burble up. I was not too surprised to discover that old Madame Chouteau, matriarch of the founding family of St. Louis, had been the first person west of the Mississippi to keep honeybees, but it was a shock to discover that as many as 50,000 cattle may have perished in Maryland, in the harsh winter of 1694–1695. In *Maryland*? Given that the first cattle only arrived on the Eastern Seaboard in 1611, that would suggest some vigorous breeding stock, besides causing one to wonder what a seventeenth-century Maryland cowboy would have looked like.

The focus on Native American life is both sharper and more extended in this new edition. An entry for Ácoma pueblo—one of the oldest continuously inhabited communities on the North American continent—is on the first page, and a discussion of the Zuni people is on the last. Policy, legislation, urban history, the environment, industrial history, and military matters are all done well. Writers are done poorly, so poorly, indeed, that one wonders whether the editor wouldn't have been better off adopting the old method, in which tiny photographs of ten or twelve writers were squeezed onto a page, allowing the reader to choose on the basis of looks.

In a remarkable and perhaps unconscious obeisance to popular taste it is the gunfighters who are done best of all, in crisp essays written with energy and finesse, and an attention to detail that exceeds what one gets for presidents, Indian chiefs, or anyone else. We learn, for example, that it was Jim Younger's "jaw" that was shot away in the Northfield, Minnesota, raid, and that Jesse James was standing on a chair straightening a picture when the assassin Robert Ford shot him down. The major shootists—the Earps, Doc Holliday, John Wesley Hardin, Hickok, Billy the Kid—get thorough and leisurely reconsiderations, in entries free of the boilerplate that is apt to be laid on for territorial governors or railroad magnates. The tug of the dime novel seems to extend even to the groves of Ivy.

The New Encyclopedia is an informative and useful book, but it's possible to read every word of it without acquiring a very clear sense of where, exactly, the contributors think the American West *is*. In part this vagueness is natural, since historically there have been several Wests. Once—as many entries acknowledge—the West began at the Atlantic beaches. By the time of Daniel Boone (1734–1820) it had moved beyond the Cumberland Gap. To Lewis and Clark it was the trans-Mississippi, though later explorers seemed to feel they weren't really in the West until they crossed the 100th Meridian. It's been nowhere clearly stated that when we talk about the West we may be talking about three entities at once: the historical West, the geographic West, and the psychological West, or what one might call the West-in-the-mind's-eye. These three Wests are interwoven in patterns that are confusing and indistinct, though the Goetzmanns, William H. and William N., came close to achieving a conscious synthesis of the three entities in their book *The West of the Imagination*, a study of western art and its reception in the East, which had first been a PBS series. No matter how hard historians try to focus on the historic West or the geographic West, the West-in-the-mind's-eye subtly but almost invariably intrudes.

For this we have the camera to thank. As soon as images became easily reproduced, and thus movable, certain cities, countries, regions became, for export purposes, reduced to one building, landmark, symbol: for China the Great Wall, for Egypt the Pyramids, for London Big Ben, for Paris the Eiffel Tower, for Moscow the Kremlin, and for the American West Monument Valley. John Ford, by setting several of his best westerns in Monument Valley—even though the stories they were telling were supposedly occurring in Texas, Arizona, or elsewhere—simply made Monument Valley stand for the West, a position since adopted by the makers of Jeep commercials and hundreds of others needing a particularly compelling site. John Ford knew quite well that, far from being representative of the West,

Monument Valley, in northern Arizona and southern Utah, was unique, not only in the West but in the world. Nowhere else are such noble buttes spaced so grandly across a red desert. But Ford insisted that the valley was as much West as was necessary, at least for what he liked to call his "pictures," and he got his way to such an extent that Monument Valley is now, for many millions, what they think of when they think about the West.

Virtually from the time cameras became portable, good photographers—Hillers, Jackson, O'Sullivan—began to work in the West, drawn by the skies, the space, and the extraordinary light. These photographers, like the many who followed them, were naturally attracted to the places of spectacular beauty: Yosemite, Yellowstone, the Canyon de Chelly, the Grand Canyon. The public, looking at these pictures year after year, became accustomed to seeing beauty shots, the glorious rather than the workaday West. When Richard Avedon published his stark *In the American West* (1985) he was greeted with howls of indignation. Where were the beauty shots? Where was Monument Valley?

Most of us, without particularly meaning to, have by now accumulated—from commercials, from ads in magazines, from picture books, from movies—a mental archive of images of the West, a personal West-in-the-mind's-eye in which we see an eternal pastoral, very beautiful but usually unpeopled, except for the Marlboro Man. These potent images, pelting us decade after decade, finally implant notions about how the West is that are as unrealistic as those of the dime novelists.

If, on the other hand, we go to photography for information, rather than fantasy, we can learn a great deal about what life was like for people who actually lived in the West, for whom those great spaces were usually just isolating and that fine light often just brutal. The photographic resources for the study of western life are very rich but also very disordered. I habitually page through all the new reference books just to see if any new pictures have turned up—and they do. In

Richard White's *New History* there is a photograph of Red Cloud's bedroom, which contained a madonna, four American flags, and a bow. I had long wondered what the great Panhandle cattleman Charles Goodnight's first wife looked like—Mary Ann Goodnight, the woman who followed him into the wilderness. She is not pictured in any of the many books that mention Goodnight, but, suddenly, there she is, smack in the middle of one of the Time-Life books, looking like a woman who could very well hold her own with Big Charlie. More than a century has now passed since the closing of the frontier, but the attics and scrapbooks of America are still yielding treasures. I myself recently turned up several new images of Geronimo, on glass-plate negatives that had been used to insulate a house in Henrietta, Texas, a small town not far from Fort Sill, where he was held. From such caprice knowledge slowly accumulates; details, little by little, get filled in.

Perhaps the last person who could confidently review a full-grown encyclopedia was C.K. Ogden, who, in 1925, took up the latest *Britannica* and found it wanting. *The New Encyclopedia* could, more modestly and just as accurately, have been called a "Handbook" or possibly a "Companion," sparing those who review it the embarrassment of having to pretend to be know-it-alls. Encyclopedias are perhaps by their nature uneven and always make tempting targets, as Diderot found out to his annoyance. Reviewing such works becomes, usually, a matter of crochets, hobbyhorses, prejudices; the editors always seem to omit the one thing the reviewer actually knows something about.

I would have liked to see an entry for *aridity*, which is, after all, the single most important climatic factor in most of the West; though mentioned time and again it could have earned an entry of its own, and the same goes for *erosion*, without which we wouldn't have had the Grand Canyon, Monument Valley, or many another emblematic sight. I'm glad to see the Creek artist Woodrow Crombo get his due but feel it's a pity that Korczak Ziolkowski and his dedicated family, now at about the midpoint of their effort to turn a mountain in South Dakota into a monument to Crazy Horse, had to be squeezed into two sentences in the entry for the Black Hills. When the Crazy Horse Monument is finished, sometime toward the middle of this century, it will be the largest sculpture on earth, and it is, already, a work of extraordinary power. A bit more of a hurrah for the Ziolkowskis wouldn't have been amiss.

The mini-bibliographies, though necessarily brief, seem unnecessarily tilted toward the monographic as opposed to the literary. Stegner's *Beyond the Hundredth Meridian* is not in the bibliography for John Wesley Powell, Evan S. Connell Jr.'s brilliant *Son of the Morning Star* not mentioned under either Custer or the Little Bighorn, and Robert Caro not mentioned under Lyndon Johnson.

In 1989, just before all these new works on the West began to appear, the University of North Carolina came forth with a massive book called *The Encyclopedia of Southern Culture*—massive and impressively thorough. There is an entry for grits, an entry for chitterlings (or chitlins), an entry for the mint julep, and such comprehensive coverage of violence that it has to be discussed under more than thirty headings.

Should there be another edition of *The New Encyclopedia of the American West* I hope the westerners in New Haven take a few tips from their cousins in Chapel Hill. For the letter C alone I can suggest two additions, the first being *chili*. In this increasingly secular age, what to put in chili—or what to exclude—provokes the nearest thing to religious argument to be heard in the modern West, while the great chili cookout held annually in Terlingua, Texas, is a loose equivalent of the Council of Nicea, in which many heresies are defined and many schismatics cast out.

I would also propose an entry for *car wrecks, fatal*. Though car wrecks happen everywhere, in the West death on the highway is as much a part of the culture as rodeos. Among writers they've carried off Walter Prescott Webb, Wallace Stegner, and Nathanael West; to car wrecks the movies have lost James Dean, Tom Mix, F. W. Murnau, Jayne Mansfield, and Sam Kinison. A little study would reveal many others, including Chato, the Chiricahua leader who helped General Crook find Geronimo, killed in a bad smash-up in New Mexico, in 1934.

Meanwhile there is still the West that was—with its achievement and its destruction—and the land that is, emptier and emptier on the plains, more and more weighed down with population on the Gulf and West Coasts, and, always, that other, endlessly imagined West, the West that can never be fully believed or wholly denied, where Wild Bird liberates Pittsburgh, where *les peaux-rouges* still bite the dust of Monument Valley, where buttes are tall and horizons long, where women mainly try to stay out of the way, and where an unforgettable company, Gene and Roy, Butch and Sundance, Clint and the Duke, wild bunches galore, and a masked man who kills the bad guys with silver bullets, still gallop from commercial to commercial on some screen somewhere, every day. That's the West that even the most accurate scholarship can't do a thing about.

Chapter 2

INVENTING THE WEST

1.

Way back yonder in 1983 Eric Hobsbawm and Terence Ranger edited an illuminating collection of studies called *The Invention of Tradition*.[1] In his introduction Professor Hobsbawm plunges right into the task at hand:

> Nothing appears more ancient, and linked to an immemorial past than the pageantry which surrounds the British monarchy in its public ceremonial manifestations. Yet, as a chapter in this book establishes, in its modern form it is the product of the late nineteenth and twentieth centuries. "Traditions" which appear or claim to be old are often quite recent in origin and sometimes invented.

A few pages later Hugh Trevor-Roper is similarly blunt in dealing with the Highland tradition of Scotland:

> Today, whenever Scotchmen gather together to celebrate their national identity, they assert it openly by certain distinctive

1. Cambridge University Press, 1983.

> national apparatus. They wear the kilt, whose color and pattern indicates their "clan"; and if they indulge in music, their instrument is the bagpipe. This apparatus, to which they ascribe great antiquity, is in fact largely modern. It was developed after, sometimes long after, the Union with England against which it is, in a sense, a protest. Before the Union, it did indeed exist in vestigial form; but that form was regarded by the large majority of Scotchmen as a sign of barbarism: the badge of roguish, idle, predatory, blackmailing Highlanders who were more of a nuisance than a threat to civilized historic Scotland.

Whoa. Several historians then proceed to march around the empire that once was, shattering immemorialist pretensions as readily as the great markswoman Annie Oakley shattered the glass balls tossed for her at Buffalo Bill's Wild West and Congress of Rough Riders of the World.

I thought, when I read *The Invention of Tradition*, that if these scholars ever turned their attention to the "traditions" of the American West there would soon be nothing left but the Golden Gate Bridge. But of course we don't need to import tradition-busters. We have Yale for that: the many eminent graduates of its American studies program have spent the last half-century turning Old West "traditions" inside out, with a certain amount of help from discontented souls at other schools.

Before Professor Hobsbawm really settles down to work he has this to say about the basic nature of some of the "traditions" which he and his colleagues will soon be reducing to rubble:

> The object and characteristic of "traditions," including invented ones, is invariance. The past, real or invented, to which they refer imposes fixed, (normally formalized) practices, such as repetition.

It's a sad, but, to my mind, inescapable fact that most of the traditions which we associate with the American West were invented by pulp writers, poster artists, impresarios, and advertising men; excepting, mainly, those that were imported from Mexico, whose *vaqueros* had about a three-century jump on our cowboys when it came to handling cattle. I don't know at exactly what point a skill becomes a "tradition," or equipment and apparel (ropes, wide-brimmed hats) become "apparatus," but many of the skills associated with American cowboys were Mexican skills moved north and adapted to Anglo-Saxon capabilities and needs. Now, pulp fiction lacks much, but it doesn't lack what Professor Hobsbawm calls invariance. (The editors of *Ranch Romances* would just call it the formula.)

As it happens there was an incident—a tragic incident—in the career of the famous nineteenth-century frontiersman Kit Carson which illustrates what can happen when an "invented" tradition and stark, uninvented reality collide. Kit Carson—a guide, but a very superior guide—was one of the most famous Americans of the nineteenth century. Buffalo Bill Cody named his only son after Kit Carson; there was a movie about Carson's exploits as early as 1904. The movie was ephemeral, and so was Carson's great work as a guide for John C. Frémont, Stephen Watts Kearny, and others. Today it would be hard to scare up one hundred Americans who could say with any accuracy what Kit Carson actually did, and ninety-five of those would be Navajos, who remember with bitterness that in 1863 he evicted their great-grandparents from their homes and marched them to an unhealthy place called the Bosque Redondo, where many of them died.

Kit, whose efforts on behalf of Frémont are well described in David Roberts's new book, *A Newer World: Kit Carson, John C. Frémont, and the Claiming of the American West*,[2] had become a dime-novel hero as early as 1847–1848, by which time he had

2. Simon and Schuster, 2000.

already managed to keep Frémont alive through three difficult expeditions.

In the fall of 1849, however, real life and the dime novel smacked into each other with a force that Kit Carson would never forget. A man named James M. White was traveling with his family on the Santa Fe Trail when they were attacked by a raiding party of Jicarilla Apaches, who killed James White and carried off Mrs. White, her child, and a servant. Pursuit was not immediate, but pursuit was eventually joined. Kit Carson lived nearby and was asked to help. In the brief autobiography which he dictated in 1856 he says that the trail was the most difficult he had ever been asked to follow; but, near the Canadian River, the rescuers finally caught up with the raiders. Carson charged immediately but was called back. The commanding officer, Captain Grier, had been told that the Apaches wanted to parley. They didn't. After taking a shot or two at the soldiers, they killed Mrs. White and fled. Here is the scene in Carson's words:

> There was only one Indian in camp, he running into the river hard by was shot. In about two hundred yards the body of Mrs. White was found, perfectly warm, had not been killed more than five minutes, shot through the heart with an arrow....
>
> In the camp was found a book, the first of the kind that I had ever seen, in which I was made a great hero, slaying Indians by the hundreds and I have often thought that Mrs. White would read the same and knowing that I lived near, she would pray for my appearance and that she might be saved. I did come but I had not the power to convince *those that were in command over me* to pursue my plan for her rescue.... [my italics]

Kit Carson was illiterate. He could sign and perhaps recognize his name, but all his life he took orders—often foolish and sometimes barbarous orders—from his superiors: men who could read.

He was never insubordinate. The dime novel found next to Mrs. White's still-warm corpse had to be read to him, or summarized. He was long haunted by the hopes that had been raised by that dime novel, hopes he had just failed to fulfill. Except for recording the fact that he married Josefa Jaramillo, his "Little Jo," Mrs. James M. White is the only woman mentioned by name in his autobiography.

2.

A year or two after reading *The Invention of Tradition* I compiled, for my own amusement, a long list of people who had a hand in inventing the West. I lost the list but remember that it began with Thomas Jefferson and ended with Andy Warhol, the latter for his *Double Elvis*, in which the King appears as a gunfighter. In between came gunmakers, boot makers, saddlemakers, railroad magnates, painters, Indians, actors, directors, liars of many descriptions, but not, by golly, very many writers: only Ned Buntline, Zane Grey, Max Brand, and Louis L'Amour. In influence, probably the most important of these was Buntline (Edward Zane Carroll Judson). It used to be said that all Russian literature came out from under Gogol's *Overcoat*; by the same, if sillier token, incalculable reams of American pulp followed from Buntline's model, and, along the way, he had as much to do as anyone with persuading a skilled buffalo hunter and middle-grade scout named William F. Cody to become the actor (later impresario) Buffalo Bill.

My old list actually served to make a simple point: the *selling* of the West preceded the *settling* of it, sometimes narrowly but other times by decades. In *The West of the Imagination*,[3] the Goetzmanns *père et fils* some years ago made this point in relation to art, but it can

3. Norton, 1986.

bear a wider application. As early as 1843—five years before Buffalo Bill was born and just about the time the Plains Indians were beginning to be alarmed by the numbers of immigrants plodding west along the Platte River—the farseeing P. T. Barnum stabled a small herd of buffalo in Hoboken. When he had them chased, for the amusement of huge crowds, some of the buffalo, not realizing that they were actors, took the whole thing too seriously and ran off into a swamp. Sometime later Barnum teamed up with James "Grizzly" Adams, who eventually succumbed to too close an association with bears, but not before he had ridden a specimen named General Fremont down Broadway.

It was quickly evident to Barnum and Buntline that the West could be made to yield a popular culture bonanza; it only needed to be promoted intelligently, and, for a time, before some of his bad tendencies, such as the one for bigamy, began to create problems, Buntline *did* promote it intelligently. By the middle of the nineteenth century he and his colleagues had the dime novel; what they needed next was the movie camera, so that all that pulp fiction could be converted into pulp film. Then all the dime novelists could start turning out scenarios, and be paid by the week instead of by the word.

Fortunately, during the long wait for the movie camera, the nation had a few other things to deal with: the Civil War, the repeal of slavery, abolition, Reconstruction, financial panics, the building of the railroads, Mark Twain, the Gilded Age, and, *still*, the Indians of the plains and deserts, those noisy barriers to the rapid suburbanization of the country.

Meanwhile show business, perhaps most notably in the long career of Buffalo Bill Cody, did its best. The researches of Cody's most substantial biographer, Don Russell,[4] have now been acutely fleshed out, particularly in iconography, by Joy S. Kasson in *Buffalo Bill's Wild West:*

4. In *The Lives and Legends of Buffalo Bill* (University of Oklahoma Press, 1960).

Celebrity, Memory, and Popular History.[5] In sheer celebrity, probably the dominant "western" figures in the last quarter of the nineteenth century were Custer, Cody, and Theodore Roosevelt, with the great resistants Sitting Bull and Geronimo in the permanent but prominent opposition, and with Sitting Bull's Little Sure Shot, Annie Oakley—who had rarely been west of Cincinnati, except to perform—representing the Western Girl. (She acted in a melodrama of that name in 1902.)

The impulse of scholars such as Joy Kasson, and also of curators, to go to the iconography—usually that means the advertising art—rather than the autobiographies of these heroes is certainly wise. Speaking of Cody, Kasson says that his autobiography "confounds easy distinctions between fact and fiction," a polite formulation that allows her to avoid saying that it's a pack of lies; as much could also be said for the self-promotional meanderings of Custer, Theodore Roosevelt, and many another westerner or pseudo-westerner. All of them, without hesitation, "confound easy distinctions between fact and fiction."

Besides being a prolific dime novelist, Ned Buntline was also a fair talent-spotter. He saw right away that the young army scout Bill Cody had theatrical potential. For one thing, Cody had an easy way with grandees. In the late 1860s he began to be called on to organize celebrity hunts—killing buffalo was then the rage. When Grand Duke Alexis of Russia showed up in the West in 1872, expecting to shoot a buffalo, Cody's skills were indispensable, the Grand Duke being, to put it mildly, no marksman. By some accounts the Grand Duke was so myopic that he shot two or three horses before they could get him pointed toward the buffalo. Cody's own account of this awkward hunt was of course more discreet, but he does admit that he had to lend the Grand Duke his best horse and his favorite rifle (called Lucrezia Borgia) and do everything but pull the trigger for him before a buffalo could be induced to fall—and he may even have pulled the trigger.

5. Hill and Wang, 2000.

The Grand Duke showed up in January. Before the year was out Buntline had Cody and a fellow army scout named Texas Jack Omohundro on the stage in Chicago, in a play called *Scouts of the Prairie*. When the action faltered Buntline enlivened things by delivering temperance lectures. The reviews were scathing, and yet people came. Where else, after all, could they see real scouts playing actors playing unreal scouts? For the next few years Cody, and sometimes Texas Jack too, commuted between their summer jobs with the army and their winter work as thespians.

Then Custer fell and Cody rushed off to help avenge him, almost immediately stumbling into some of the best publicity of his whole career, his famous "duel" with the Cheyenne warrior Hay-o-wei, or Yellow Hair (usually mistranslated as Yellow Hand). This occurred on July 17, 1876—about three weeks after the Little Bighorn. Even with a Hinman collator it would not be easy to sort out the numerous versions of this "duel." Various others who were in the field that day felt that they might have been the one to kill Yellow Hair. Probably Cody shot him—certainly he scalped him, taking the famous "first scalp for Custer"—the last, too, for a while.

Cody, whose touch with women was never as sure as his touch with horses, promptly sent this grisly trophy to his wife, Louisa, from whom he was mostly absent and usually estranged. Thanks to some miracle of the nineteenth-century mail, the scalp reached Mrs. Cody before she even knew that Yellow Hair was dead, or, for that matter, that he had ever lived.

Matters never really improved between Bill and Louisa. Some years later, after his first triumphs in Europe, Cody foolishly sued her for divorce, and lost. It was revealed in depositions that the woman Mrs. Cody was most jealous of was Queen Victoria—an eligible widow, after all. The Queen didn't seem to be *that* charmed by Cody, but she did admire an Indian named Red Shirt, who gets mentioned in her diary. For a time Cody conducted an expensive flirtation with an actress named Katherine Clemmons, who soon married Jay Gould's son. Memory of this frustration caused Cody to declare that he would rather manage a million Indians than one soubrette.

3.

When he died, Annie Oakley, whom Cody always called Little Missie (despite the fact that she was, for fifty years, a married woman), had this to say:

> I traveled with him for seventeen years. There were thousands of men in the outfit during that time, Comanches, cowboys, Cossacks, Arabs, and every kind of person. And the whole time we were one great family loyal to one man. His words were better than most contracts. Personally I never had a contract with the show once I started. It would have been superfluous.

Kit Carson said of his own autobiography that he thought the folks who wrote it down had "laid it on a leetle thick," and Little Missie was certainly laying it on a "leetle thick" here. She did have contracts and her relations with the Colonel, as she called him, were not always serene. Not long before the big European tour Cody—with his usual flawed comprehension of women—presented Annie with a rival, a chubby fifteen-year-old California markswoman named Lillian Smith. Annie Oakley immediately lopped six years off her own age, and later performed for a season with Cody's sometime partner, sometime rival Pawnee Bill (Gordon Lillie).

Few of Cody's managers or business partners would have agreed with Little Missie about the quality of his word, either—if only because he could rarely remember very accurately what he had agreed to. The selection of his business correspondence, *The Business of Being Buffalo*

Bill: Selected Letters of William F. Cody, 1879–1917,[6] edited by Sarah Jo Blackstone, suggested that his attention to contractual details was likely, at best, to be momentary. Few of the letters are more than a paragraph long. The troupe he managed was enormous, with sometimes as many as seven hundred people and lots of animals. It took fifty railroad cars to transport them. Like most show business troupes, Buffalo Bill's had good seasons and not-so-good seasons. By the 1890s, when Wild West shows were at the height of their popularity, there were two or three dozen troupes large and small wandering around America—and the world. When Henry Adams and his friend John Lafarge set out on their big trip to the South Seas in 1890 they shared their boat with a Wild West troupe bound for Australia. The field was never Cody's alone.

Usually, though, Cody had the most Indians. For all his overstated prowess as an Indian fighter Cody, in the main, liked Indians and a good many Indians respected him. Like many another old scout he may have realized that at bottom he had more in common with the Indians than he did with the dandies and the swells. In 1872, with the Plains wars by no means over, Cody persuaded Spotted Tail, leader of the Brulé Sioux and uncle of Crazy Horse, to bring some warriors and cut up a little for Grand Duke Alexis. From the first he used Indians in the Wild West shows, and he sometimes had to fight the Department of the Interior to do it. The government didn't want Indians to get to show off. The never predictable Sioux historian Vine Deloria Jr. thinks it was a good thing for Indians to be in the Wild West shows: it beat staying home and being harassed by the government. The question of their participation has now been thoroughly studied, both by Joy Kasson and by L. G. Moses in *Wild West Shows and the Images of American Indians, 1883–1933.*[7]

6. Praeger, 1988.

7. University of New Mexico Press, 1996.

When Cody took his troupe to England for Queen Victoria's Golden Jubilee in 1887, he took ninety-seven Indians with him, including Black Elk, the Sioux visionary, who mentioned that Queen Victoria's hand was little and soft. He also said that Pawhuska (Cody) had a great heart. Sitting Bull was a harder case. Cody called him "peevish"—one of his few understatements—and managed to keep him with the Wild West show only one year, 1885. When Sitting Bull left Cody gave him a horse and a hat, both of which he kept until his death, five years later.

From the mid-1880s into the new century, Cody, despite persistent rivals such as Doc Carver and Pawnee Bill, was probably the most prominent purveyor of western "traditions." Custer had flamed out in 1876, his death being his most glorious career move, though, for his troops, it was just death. In the Eighties Theodore Roosevelt produced his *Winning of the West*, as romantic a history as one could want. The West pretty much *had* been won by then, if "won" is the right word. Roosevelt was also just completing his three-year flirtation with ranching in the Dakotas—in *Mornings on Horseback* David McCullough reckons that T. R. was actually *in* the West only a little more than a year.[8] A while later, when he got ready to make war on Spain, T. R. borrowed the concept of Rough Riders from Cody's show, and Cody responded by promptly reenacting the Battle of San Juan Hill.

William F. Cody's "invention," begun with a nudge from Ned Buntline and developed with the help of his long-suffering assistants Nate Salsbury and John Burke, was to take the kind of pageants current in Barnum and others and focus them on the West, the winning of which thus came to seem a triumphant *national* venture. The audiences not only bought it, they loved it, at least as long as Cody was there himself, on his white horse. What his career proved is that there is almost no limit to how far a man can go in America if he looks

8. Simon and Schuster, 1981.

good on a horse; and Buffalo Bill looked so good on a horse that it was almost as if the animal had been created just for him to ride. T. R. by contrast *never* looked good on a horse—on a horse he just looked impatient. He looked a little better with a gun, particularly if he happened to be standing by a large dead animal which he had just killed.

Like Mark Twain and Ulysses S. Grant, Cody was a fool with money. He sunk a bunch of it into something called White Beaver's Laugh Cream, the Great Lung Healer, an herbal remedy which arrived on the market roughly a century too soon. The movie camera finally arrived—Annie Oakley went before it in 1894—but it didn't really improve matters for Cody. He invested much money, time, and energy in an "authentic" western called *The Indian Wars* (1913) which flopped. In 1916 he was forced to seek employment with the Miller Brothers, owners of the famous 100,000-acre 101 Ranch in Oklahoma, who for some years—1905 to 1925 particularly—ran a successful Wild West show in addition to their cattle business. In 1916 the Millers were recovering from a bit of bad timing: an attempted tour of Europe in the fall of 1914. They got to England and promptly had almost all their livestock requisitioned by the British; a lot of half-broken Mexican cow ponies that the Millers had bought on the cheap in Mexico saw service in France. Somehow the Millers got everybody home, including, even, a band of Oglala Sioux who had been farmed out to a circus and happened to be in Germany when war broke out. With Buffalo Bill on board the Millers tried to run a tour under a rather labored title: "Buffalo Bill (Himself) and the 101 Ranch Wild West Combined with the Military Pageant of Preparedness."

The whole story of the Millers and the 101 Ranch—at one point they employed Tom Mix, and Will Rogers enjoyed dropping by—has been well told by Michael Wallis in *The Real Wild West: The 101 Ranch and the Creation of the American West*.[9] He gives a good account of

9. St. Martin's, 1999.

another of the Millers' foreign imbroglios, this one in Mexico City. The Millers bet that their star cowboy, the black bulldogging champion Bill Pickett, could hold his own for five minutes with a fighting bull named Frijoles Chiquitos. Pickett won the bet for his bosses, staying in the ring with Frijoles Chiquitos for thirty-eight minutes, seven and a half of which were spent clinging to the animal's horns.

As far as the bull and the bulldogger went, the contest was a standoff: Pickett couldn't throw the bull and the bull couldn't gore Pickett. But the crowd, outraged by this insult to their bull, all but rioted. Pickett was eventually conked by a bottle thrown from the stands, but all escaped. Even Bill Pickett's favorite horse, Spradley, who had been gored in the fracas, survived, thanks to the mysterious intervention of an old Mexican man who wandered up and thrust a red banana deep into Spradley's wound, curing him almost immediately. Bill Pickett, at the time, was earning eight dollars a week and board for putting himself and Spradley to this trouble.

When William F. Cody died, in 1917, he proved not to have been able to control even his own corpse. He had chosen a burial spot in Cody, Wyoming, but his current partner, Harry Tammen, the Denver newspaperman, either bullied or bamboozled the grieving Louisa and had the Last of the Great Scouts put to rest on Lookout Mountain, near Denver.

4.

Annie Oakley (Phoebe Ann Moses—or Mosey) grew up poor in rural Ohio, shot game to feed her family, shot game to sell, was pressed into a shooting contest with a touring sharpshooter named Frank Butler, beat him, married him, stayed with him for fifty years, and died three weeks before he did in 1926.

When Annie Oakley and Frank Butler offered themselves to Cody the Colonel was dubious. His fortunes were at a low ebb, and shooting acts abounded. But he gave Annie Oakley a chance. She walked out in Louisville before 17,000 people and was hired immediately. Nate Salsbury, Cody's tight-fisted manager, who did not spend lavishly and who rarely highlighted performers, happened to watch Annie rehearse and promptly ordered seven thousand dollars' worth of posters and billboard art.

Annie Oakley more than justified the expense. Sitting Bull, normally a taciturn fellow, saw her shoot in Minnesota and could not contain himself. *Watanya cicilia*, he called her, his Little Sure Shot. Small, reserved, Quakerish, she seemed to live on the lemonade Buffalo Bill dispensed free to all hands. In London she demolished protocol by shaking hands with Princess Alexandra. She shook hands with Alexandra's husband, the Prince of Wales, too, though, like his mother the Queen, she strongly disapproved of his behavior with the ladies. In France the Parisians were glacially indifferent to buffalo, Indians, cowboys, and Cody—Annie Oakley melted them so thoroughly that she had to go through her act five times before she could escape. In Germany she likened Bismarck to a mastiff.

In 1901 she was almost killed in a train wreck. Annie claimed that it was the wreck that caused her long auburn hair to turn white overnight; skeptics said her hair turned white because she left it in hot water too long while at a spa. She continued to shoot into the 1920s. In her last years she looked rather like Nancy Astor. Will Rogers visited her not long before her death and pronounced her the perfect woman. Probably not until Billie Jean King and the rise of women's tennis had a female outdoor performer held the attention of so many people. She became part of the "invention" that is the West by winning her way with a gun: a man's thing, the very thing, in fact, that had won the West itself.[10]

---

10. See Glenda Riley, *The Life and Legacy of Annie Oakley* (University of Oklahoma Press, 1994) and Isabelle S. Sayers, *Annie Oakley and Buffalo Bill's Wild West* (Dover, 1981).

As the frontier closed odd liaisons formed and strange dislocations occurred. Sitting Bull, in the last year of his life, took Katherine Weldon, a gentlewoman from Brooklyn, into his home on the Standing Rock reservation. Indian agent James McLaughlin, who disliked and distrusted Sitting Bull, assured his superiors that the relationship wasn't "criminal," but he may have been wrong.

Will Rogers saw Buffalo Bill's Wild West in Chicago in 1893 and was fascinated by the trick roping of Vicente Oropeza. Back home, young Will began to practice with the rope, but his first best chance to perform came in South Africa where, just after the Boer War, he had gone to deliver a load of Argentine livestock. The impresario who hired him was Texas Jack Jr., the namesake of Buffalo Bill's old scouting crony, Texas Jack Omohundro. Young Rogers, soon to be so famous, performed some of his first rope tricks for an audience that—according to his biographer Ben Yagoda—at one point included Mohandas Gandhi, then a lawyer in Johannesburg.

Later, when he was the best-paid performer at Twentieth Century Fox, Rogers lived on his ranch in Pacific Palisades, entertaining such immortals as Charlie Chaplin, Paulette Goddard, and, one evening, Will Durant; the historian of civilization was happy to report to his wife, Ariel, that he had been picked up in a "nifty Cadillac." Around this time Will Rogers made a remark that goes straight to the heart of the selling of the West: "The more you do anything that don't look like advertising the better advertising it is."[11]

In my view the main reason the Old West became so enormously popular as entertainment was that the great engines of the media were well stoked before the actual settling was even half completed. Consider Billy the Kid. In real terms he was a minor outlaw: many did worse. But the name was catchy and the media was ready; Billy's

11. See Ben Yagoda, *Will Rogers* (University of Oklahoma Press, 2000).

bibliography now exceeds five thousand items, and they are still coming.

If we apply Professor Hobsbawm's notion of invariance to the invented traditions of the Old West, we might conclude that only the pulpers and the advertising men have held a strict course. John Ford, in *The Man Who Shot Liberty Valance*, varied the formula, a little. Clint Eastwood, in *Unforgiven*, finally varied the formula, a little. But Louis L'Amour, through one hundred and twenty books, held to his formula as tightly as Bill Pickett held to the deadly horns of Frijoles Chiquitos. And so do the Marlboro ads: always the same horses, the same hills, the same ropes, the same handsome guys.

William F. Cody's frantic efforts, toward the end of his life, to make an "authentic" western about the Indian wars may have been a sad effort to grasp again, somehow, the reality that had been there when he was young. The old man of sixty-seven rescalped for the camera the Cheyenne Hay-o-wei, whom he had *really* scalped in July of 1876. Cody had by then spent more than forty years peddling illusions about the West, and now he wanted the reality back so that Americans who would never see a free Indian could know what the winning of the West had "really" been like. But the killing of Hay-o-wei itself happened because of the sunburst of publicity generated by Custer's death. The papers wanted more, and they wanted it soon. When Cody did it again for the cameras, thirty-seven years later, the venture flopped. By that time it was Cody himself, not the American audiences, who wanted the reality back. Americans, now as then, were perfectly happy with the illusion—only, if you would please, try not to let the advertising show.

Chapter 3

CHOPPING DOWN THE SACRED TREE

It takes a bold paleface to attempt a comprehensive history of Native American life nowadays—after being forced to swallow five hundred years of insulting and mainly inaccurate Anglo-European generalizations about their character and behavior, the Native Americans are justifiably tetchy. Get it wrong and Russell Means, the activist-turned-actor who has managed to play both the last of the Mohicans (Chingachgook, in Michael Mann's adaptation of James Fenimore Cooper's novel) and the fiercest of the Sioux (Sitting Bull, in my own *Buffalo Girls*) might show up on your doorstep, wearing his big hat; or Vine Deloria Jr., the unmellowed Sioux polemicist, might launch a lightning bolt or two, possibly from that bastion of nativism, the Op-Ed page of *The New York Times*; or the young rumbler from the Northwest, Sherman Alexie, anointed by *Granta* as one of the twenty best young American writers of 1999, might pop onto one of the paleface talk shows and complain.

The fact is, the natives are right to rumble; in any consideration of their history there is a very great deal to be got wrong, and conceptual problems abound, the commonest of which I have myself encountered while about the prosaic task of screenwriting. A producer or studio may have the notion that they want a movie about Geronimo, but it will always develop that what they really want is a movie about the white guys who were *chasing* Geronimo—maybe one of them could be Brad Pitt. In a broad sense, as it is with the movies, so it has been with history. Native American history becomes, in a flash, not *their* history, but the history of Anglo-European interaction with them, on two continents and a number of adjacent islands. The rest of the story—I would think, from a Native American point of view it would be the deep story—is left for archaeologists, anthropologists, paleontologists, ethnobotanists, and, always, the singers, the storytellers, the poets.

Some idea of the dimensions of the history James Wilson attempts to cram into the 466 pages of *The Earth Shall Weep: A History of Native America*[1] might be suggested by the fact that the admirable Civilization of the American Indian series, published by the University of Oklahoma over almost seventy years, now numbers some two hundred and twenty volumes; the more specialized bulletins of the Bureau of American Ethnology are also in the hundreds. The geographical area to be covered, if one attempts to tell the whole story, stretches from the Atlantic to the Pacific and from the Arctic Ocean to the Straits of Magellan, a huge amount of ground to survey, or dig in—and hundreds are even now digging.

Every year, it seems, some new old bones turn up in Oregon or Chile that seem to push the arrival date of the Native Americans farther and farther back into prehistory. An exciting new find in Tenochtitlan was announced while I was reading Mr. Wilson's book. Of the hundreds of questions that might be asked about Native American history, very few have definitive answers. Did Clovis man, with his excellent spearpoints, kill and eat all the woolly mammoths that once roamed the Great Plains, much as buffalo hunters with excellent bullets later almost wiped out the buffalo? Or did the great beasts merely get frozen in an ice age? How many Native Americans

---

1. Atlantic Monthly Press, 1999.

were there when the Europeans arrived, and what percentage of them were dead one hundred years later? Who made the great designs in the Atacama Desert of South America, designs so large that they could not have been wholly seen by their creators but only by soaring birds, the immortal gods, or twentieth-century humans in airplanes? What happened to the peoples of Mesa Verde or Chaco Canyon? If they left, where did they go?

James Wilson is well aware of these questions; he knows there are mysteries in Native American history that he has not solved or even probed. He has written a personal history—it might better have been called a reflection on that history—and brings to the task intelligence, passion, and sympathy, all attributes that would have been better served if, in view of the magnitude of the topic, he had produced a less hasty listing of sources, so that some of the statements he makes could have been handily checked. Early on, for example, he says there may be human artifacts in Mexico that are as much as 200,000 years old. Perhaps there are, but the figure startles when applied to Mexico; it would have been helpful to track it to an archaeological reference.

It would have been useful, too, if Mr. Wilson had faced a little more critically the considerable problems posed by translation from the dozen or more far from simple language families to which the Native Americans belonged. Listen to the Cherokee Onitositah, called Corn Tassel, complaining in 1777:

> Let us examine the facts of your present irruption into our country.... What did you do? You marched into our territories with a superior force...your numbers far exceeded us, and we fled to the stronghold of our extensive woods.... Your laws extend not into our country, nor ever did....
>
> Indeed, much has been advanced on the want of what you term civilization among the Indians; and many proposals have been made to us to adopt your laws, your religion, your manners

> and your customs. But, we confess that we do not yet see the propriety, or practicability, of such a reformation, and should be better pleased with beholding the good effect of these doctrines in your own practices than with hearing you talk about them....

That sounds pretty Augustan to me; Dr. Johnson—who wouldn't have been on Corn Tassel's side—couldn't have put it better; the question it raises is why all Native American orators, whatever their language group, are translated to sound either like Dr. Johnson, the prophet Isaiah, or, at a stretch, the Sioux wise man Black Elk, himself rather fulsomely translated by the poet John G. Neihardt and his daughters.

The problem of exact translation is huge; it bedeviled native–white relations from the first. Many a native leader went home from the treaty councils believing he had heard promises that the white leaders then claimed they had never made. The writer Alex Shoumatoff recently reckoned that our government had broken 378 treaties with the Native Americans; many of those treaties bore little resemblance to what the native negotiators supposed they were agreeing to. At both the diplomatic and the personal level misunderstandings were constant.

It could be argued, for example, that Crazy Horse's death was hastened by a famous mistranslation. In 1877 the army, having just disarmed Crazy Horse, was forced to note, with embarrassment, that the undisarmed Nez Percé were racing along a clear track to Canada, whipping up on everyone who got in their way. Someone had the bad idea of rearming Crazy Horse, in hopes that he would stop them. In the course of a tedious parley Crazy Horse was reported to have said that he was prepared to live in peace, but if the whites really wanted him to fight he would fight until every last white man was dead. The interpreter who reported this statement was Frank Grouard, a mixed-blood scout who knew Crazy Horse fairly well. The army, already nervous, took Crazy Horse at what they thought was his word and soon ordered his arrest. But was it his word? Other Sioux speakers at the parley heard him say he would fight until every last Nez Percé was dead—they were aghast at Frank Grouard's mistake and tried to convince the officers that Crazy Horse hadn't said anything of the sort.

What *did* Crazy Horse say? He hated meetings; might he have said something outrageous just to get out of the tent? Was Frank Grouard drunk? Did he want to get Crazy Horse in more trouble than he was already in? Could he have genuinely misunderstood? We will never know. The incident is significant only because something similar may have occurred in hundreds of parleys, with neither side fully realizing that the interpreting was lazy, inaccurate, or biased. When spread over five hundred years of military and political engagement, linguistic imprecision is bound to have tragic results.

James Wilson is aware of the problem presented by language, as he is aware of many problems that he hasn't space to address. Issues large and small flit around his head like gnats; he swats at them now and then but his larger purpose prevents him from being able to quite dispel them. He has committed himself to taking the reader through Native American history on a bullet train and can rarely afford to ease up on the throttle. He wisely concentrates his narrative on what is now the continental United States, saying little of Canada, Mexico, or the southern continent, but, even so, he has to rush.

The train immediately plunges into the historical forests of the Northeast, allowing the reader, who had better not blink, time to glance only briefly into thickets of unfamiliar names and distant scenes: Wahunsonacock, Opechancanough, Wopigwooit, Miantonomo, Nemattanew, from the Powhatan, Pequot, Narragansett, or Pamunkey peoples. James Wilson does a fair job of summarizing the early contacts and conflicts, and wrestles manfully with the functioning of the Hotinonshonni, the complex religious, social, and political organization which allowed the six Iroquois peoples to maintain—as they still do—a sense of identity and destiny which enabled them to work together against the intruders. But as we proceed southeast, toward the country of the Five Civilized Tribes, a good many readers are apt to be overwhelmed, as this reader nearly was, by a sense of their own deep and dismal ignorance where Native American history is concerned. The unhappy truth, in regard to this history, is that we are now mostly movie-taught, if taught at all. The common reader—that elusive beast—will at most now be vaguely familiar with a thin slice of history drawn from two decades near the end of the nineteenth century, when the resistance of the native peoples of the plains and deserts was finally being broken. The battle of the Little Bighorn, in 1876, is one of the most written about battles in world history, whereas equally desperate battles in the Northeast, the Southeast, or the Ohio Valley are forgotten, an example being the battle of Horseshoe Bend, in what is now Alabama, when Andrew Jackson broke the considerable power of the Creek nation, almost losing his life in the process. (He was saved by Junaluska, a Cherokee, who had reason to regret his charity when his people, at Jackson's insistence, were dispossessed of their ancestral lands and driven westward along the Trail of Tears. According to Mr. Wilson, Junaluska even went to the White House to plead for more time—Jackson merely showed him the door.)

The difference between what we comprehend of late-nineteenth-century Native Americans, as opposed to their equally gifted forebears, boils down in the end to publicity. There was a publicity machine ready for Custer and and his determined opponents, Sitting Bull and Crazy Horse, as there was not for such extraordinary leaders as King Philip or Tecumseh. Few now would even have heard of Tecumseh, the great Shawnee who, for a time, forged a powerful alliance of native peoples, if a Civil War general, William Tecumseh Sherman, hadn't been given his name.

By the 1860s the publicity machine was even sophisticated enough to supply the native leaders with catchy, marquee-ready translations of their sometimes complex names. How much would we have read of Chief Joseph if the papers had been forced to call him Hin-mah-too-yah-lat-kekt? Or of Sitting Bull if he had required them to address him formally as Tatanka Iyotake?

James Wilson speeds on, does the Five Civilized Tribes, then the Pueblo peoples and the West Coast peoples, before curving back to the Great Plains; the landscape blurs a little at times as he races to complete his survey. The last third of the book is more reasonably paced; it deals with the struggles of the native peoples in the twentieth century, when the attacks they faced were bureaucratic rather than military. He devotes an informative chapter to the still controversial and rather quixotic career of John Collier, for eleven years FDR's commissioner of Indian affairs, who was determined to see that there was a New Deal for Native Americans too, though to many tribal peoples their New Deal still meant that the whites expected them to govern themselves in a very white manner; Collier pushed for the much-debated Indian Reorganization Act, embittering, at a stroke, many of the natives he was trying to help and all of the capitalists who didn't want him to help them. Collier, like many another sympathetic white bureaucrat, was determined to help the tribal people, but, of course, to help them *his* way; in the long struggle to implement his reforms he underestimated both the tenacity of tribal traditions and the undeviating power of capitalist greed, but he did at least manage to arrest the constant diminishment of the Native American land base.

As James Wilson nears the end of his history certain contradictory pressures begin to affect his narrative. Any honest history of Native American life over the last five centuries is essentially going to be a black book, a catalog of horrors, butcheries, exterminations. From the very first the exterminationist—we would now say genocidal—impulse was there. Large numbers of the invaders simply wanted to kill all the natives, that being the simplest and quickest way to get their land. Mr. Wilson's pages on the elimination of the Indians of northern California during the hectic decade of the gold rush can stand for many such killing frenzies. In their fevered haste to get to the diggings and become rich, many of the miners found the Indian presence intolerable; they killed them any way they could. One of the more sensitive riflemen, Mr. Wilson reports, was distressed at having to shoot Indian children with his rifle because the large bullets tore up the small corpses so badly; but he was soon able to square his conscience on this score by resolving to shoot adults with his rifle and children with his .38 revolver.

In these centuries of slaughter several themes repeat themselves, one being the inability or unwillingness of the whites to distinguish between friendly and unfriendly natives. Their practice was usually just to punish whatever Indians could be found; in some cases—here's another theme—it didn't matter much because the white man's diseases went ahead of him, wiping out friend and foe alike.

The one overriding theme, however, in every period and every region, is always land. The natives had it, the whites wanted it, and, one way or another, whether with bullet or treaty, they took it, and are still taking it today in Ecuador and Brazil, where the few remaining free indigenous peoples of the Americas are finding that there is no forest deep enough to shield them from the settlers and the oil companies. John Collier, for all his bullying, was hated by capitalists because he wanted to fix it in law that the Native Americans got to keep at least a little land.

About this James Wilson is quite clear. The natives once occupied two continents and the Europeans came and took them. And yet Mr. Wilson would like to argue that the native peoples have survived with at least their spiritual beliefs and identities intact—that they have preserved their sacramental relationship with the earth and their conviction that they live in a reciprocal universe. Despite the very convincing black book that he has produced, his desire to believe that Native

American life is now stable and even flourishing leads him to produce this curious passage about a Native American reservation he visited on the Great Plains:

> You get a sense of how tenuous the Euro-American grip is if you drive across the west today. Large swathes of the region are littered with deserted farmsteads and dying towns—crumbling stores, bars and gas stations, dilapidated little houses gradually taking on the bleached colours of the surrounding landscape—that look as if they have just been dropped there for no particular reason and then abandoned. When you cross into a Native American reservation, the communities have much the same impoverished, improvised appearance, but the atmosphere is far more vital and energetic, with bustling shops and hordes of children playing in the street. You get the unmistakable impression that, unlike their nomadic Anglo neighbours, who stay for a generation and then move on, these are people who feel they belong and have a future here.

Pardon me? Where is this model reservation town, with apparent impoverishment and an improvised appearance, yet with bustling shops? It sounds a little like downtown Berkeley, though probably all Mr. Wilson means by the bustling shops is that a tour bus happened to stop at the tribal crafts center while he was there. Doubtless the Euro-American inhabitants of such substantial paleface reservations as Denver, Omaha, Minneapolis, and Chicago would be surprised at the suggestion that their grip is tenuous and that they may soon be moving on.

Such a passage flips reality like a pancake. It was the Plains Indians who were the great nomads of the Americas and the whites who cooped them up on small reservations so that they themselves could farm what had been the nomad's prairie. What *is* to be noted on the Great

Plains today is that the white towns have become as sad as the Indian towns, but that is not a development that supports Mr. Wilson's observation. His stated task puts him in a more or less constant bind, poised uneasily between the particular and the general. He says over and over again that all tribes are particular in their customs, and yet haste forces him into generalizations such as the one just quoted, and he forgets that even tribes who are close neighbors may have lifeways that are very different. I was once invited to the Crow sundance, which was so packed with white anthropologists that year that it might as well have been held in Harvard Yard; but I was staying at the time on the nearby Cheyenne reservation, to whose sundance I would never have been invited. Between these neighboring peoples, as between many, the historical divisions are very deep. The Crow, after all, scouted for Custer, while the Cheyenne were part of the team that annihilated him, and were punished accordingly.

In 1990 the Lakota Sioux made a memorial march to the site of the massacre at Wounded Knee, the massacre which, forgetting South America, was thought to mark the end of armed hostility between whites and Native Americans. Mr. Wilson, who worked on a two-part BBC documentary about Native American life, was at Pine Ridge and interviewed some of the marchers. Since he starts his story with this march to the bleak plain where the Ghost Dancers were slaughtered, it is a pity that he doesn't deal a little more fully with Indian millenarianism itself: the belief appearing in many places that a new soil would cover the earth, cleansing the continent of whites and raising up the honored dead.

James Wilson does mention that the Pamunkey prophet Nemattanew was preaching of a Return as early as 1618. Such preachings have always made the whites nervous—what if the magic worked?—and they always overreacted to it, at Wounded Knee most famously, but also at Cibicue Creek in Arizona in 1881 when the Apache preacher Noch-ay-del-klinne was killed with eighteen of his followers, and other times as well. What the whites forget is that to poverty-stricken and despairing peoples (white or Indian) the Apocalypse has always looked good.

When he is discussing the Sioux who made the march to Wounded Knee Mr. Wilson comments that many Americans think the Indians have vanished because, well, many of them no longer look like Indians, but he does not push a discussion of the merging of races very far. It is merely one of the gnats that flit around his head, but in fact there have been five hundred years in which both blood and cultures have been mixing. When, at the turn of the twentieth century, the Dawes Commission was attempting to break down the tribal structures of the Five Civilized Tribes in order to make the tribal members American citizens, the census rolls compiled at that time only listed about a quarter of the Indians as full-bloods. How much harder would it be to find a full-blood in Oklahoma now? I have Sioux blood through my paternal grandmother but had a ranch rather than a reservation upbringing. The most gifted of the writers who are called Native American now—N. Scott Momaday, Leslie Marmon Silko, Louise Erdrich, Joy Harjo, Gerald Vizenor, Sherman Alexie, and others—have for two generations ranged widely through the white academies, from Dartmouth and Cambridge to Stanford and Seattle; they not only know what their ancestors knew as tribal people, they know what our ancestors knew as dead white Europeans. With this long mixing of bloods and cultures it is now less easy, in speaking of Native Americans, to know to what extent they are we and we they.

James Wilson earnestly seeks signs of Native American revitalization, but too often seeks it in political or social developments; if he had only looked to literature rather than politics he would have found an abundance of examples. Perhaps the most eloquent treatment of the theme of the Return—the theme Mr. Wilson seems to be looking for—is to be found in Leslie Marmon Silko's *Almanac of the*

Dead (1991), the concluding paragraphs of which I quote. Sterling, a Laguna man long exiled from his people, has come home to look at a great stone snake uncovered in a uranium mine:

> Sterling sat for a long time near the stone snake. The breeze off the juniper cooled his face and neck. He closed his eyes. The snake didn't care if people were believers or not; the work of the spirits and prophecies went on regardless. Spirit beings might appear anywhere, even near open pit mines. The snake didn't care about uranium tailings; humans had desecrated only themselves with the mine, not the earth. Burned and radioactive, with all humans dead, the earth would still be sacred. Man was too insignificant to desecrate her.
>
> Sterling didn't show himself in Laguna for a long time, and then only to buy food. He had held his breath, but the Tribal Council had ignored him.... Sterling didn't look like his old self anymore. He had lost weight and quit drinking beer. The postmaster reported Sterling had let go all his magazine subscriptions. Sterling didn't care about the rumours and the gossip because Sterling knew why the giant snake had returned now; he knew what the snake's message was to the people. The snake was looking south, in the direction from which the twin brothers and the people would come.

Ignored at the time it was published (except by Sven Birkerts, who was startled by its ambition), the *Almanac* is steadily making its way, as are the books of several other brilliant Native American writers in whose pages Mr. Wilson would find, well expressed, the evidence of the survival of spiritual identity that he is looking for.

James Wilson gives us the creation myths of a number of tribes, and lists in his sources several of the Native American writers I've named, but it is not clear that he has followed these writers into *their* stories. Black Elk, in a famous elegiac passage, said, in speaking of the Indian's defeat and demoralization, that the nation's hoop was broken and the sacred tree dead, but in the work of a number of Native American writers the sacred tree can be seen to be blossoming profusely again. Whatever their differences of tribe or talent, these writers are alike in one way: they all protect the stories of their people, in the conviction that by protecting the stories they secure not only the past but the future too.

Chapter 4

A HERONE OF THE PRAIRIES

Historians who devote their careers to the study of institutions—even a Maitland or a Namier—never enjoy the broad popularity of the chroniclers of conquest and empire (Prescott, Parkman, Macaulay, Churchill). Most people would rather read about the Goths at the gates of Rome, or Napoleon watching Moscow burn, or Kitchener at Khartoum, or Custer at the Little Bighorn, than follow Maitland as he patiently separates common law from canon law, or absorb Namier's stately reconstruction of the parliament of George III. The great historians of institutions don't scorn popularity, but the law, or parliament, come to exert such a fascination for them that they don't have time to worry about much except their charters, their pedigrees, and their lists.

So it was with the too-little-known American historian Angie Debo (1890–1988), who early made it her task to elucidate what might be called the Second Dispossession of the Five Civilized Tribes once they had been brought to the eastern part of what is now Oklahoma and settled on land that was to be theirs inalienably. This dispossession was legislative and bureaucratic rather than military, but it was no less relentless for that; and Angie Debo, in three somber and scrupulous histories published in the Thirties and early Forties, extracts the story detail by detail from congressional records, legislative acts and the amendments to legislative acts, treaties and the alteration and, finally, abrogation of treaties, from records of land tenure, allotment rolls, tribal budgets, transcripts of hearings, minutes of tribal councils, censuses, surveys, agricultural reports, tax rolls, small-town and tribal newspapers, and the mass of inadvertently damning statistics compiled, as the dispossession was taking place, by the Department of the Interior.

In the preface to *And Still the Waters Run: The Betrayal of the Five Civilized Tribes*,[1] a book whose conclusions—not to mention its naming of names—proved too volatile for it to be published in Oklahoma, Angie Debo has this to say about what was to be her chosen subject:

> Every schoolboy knows that from the settlement of Jamestown to the 1870s Indian warfare was a perpetual accompaniment to American pioneering, but the second stage of dispossession of the Indians is not so generally and romantically known. The age of military conquest was succeeded by the age of economic absorption, when the long rifle of the frontiersman was replaced by the legislative enactment and court decrees of the legal exploiter, and the lease, mortgage and deed of the land shark.

Where the Five Tribes were concerned her job, as she came to see it, was to write the history of the chiseling era; the whole of her early and most vigorous work might be taken as a gloss on the weary remark made by the Oglala chief Red Cloud in his old age:

> They made us many promises, more than I can remember, but they never kept but one; they promised to take our land, and they took it.

1. Princeton University Press, 1940.

Even her last book, the excellent biography of Geronimo published when she was eighty-six, was at bottom another history of dispossession, only this time she did have, at the center of her story, a character the public at large might want to read about.

The three books of Debo's first period, in which she tells, precisely, how the Five Tribes lost much of their new western lands, are *The Rise and Fall of the Choctaw Republic*,[2] *And Still the Waters Run*, and *The Road to Disappearance*.[3] The title of the first book describes it accurately; *And Still the Waters Run* analyzes the development and enactment (or one could say infliction) of the land allotment policy (the real heartbreaker for the Indians); and *The Road to Disappearance: A History of the Creek Indians* is a history of the Creek Confederacy until its dissolution in 1907, when Oklahoma became a state.

Read together, as a trilogy, these books represent a remarkable intellectual surge for a young woman who had been left to cool her heels, educationally, for several years, because Marshall, Oklahoma, the town she called home for eighty-nine of her eventual ninety-eight years, had no high school for her to go to. She was certified to teach in rural schools when she was sixteen but did not finish high school until she was twenty-three. When she finally got to the University of Oklahoma and chose history as her subject, she was lucky to find a mentor, Edward Everett Dale, who pointed her toward the rich and then virtually unexplored state archives, little suspecting how deeply, persistently, and provocatively she would eventually delve.

Angie Debo seems to have been one of those rare souls whose fascination from the first is with bureaucratic practice and governmental policy. At the University of Chicago (M.A., 1924) she did a thesis on American isolationist policy, got it published, and seemed pointed toward the study of international affairs, but the job market for a

2. University of Oklahoma Press, 1934, 1961.

3. University of Oklahoma Press, 1941.

young woman in that line of work proved nil. In fact, the only job she could get that allowed her to teach history at all was at tiny West Texas State Teacher's College in Canyon, a fate that led her to complain for the next sixty years about the backwardness of history departments. (She must have envied her one female predecessor in the field of Five Tribes studies, Annie Heloise Abel, born in Sussex and brought to Kansas early, who promptly doubled back to Yale, where she took a doctorate in 1905, while Angie Debo was still hoping for a high school.)

When Angie Debo was teaching in Canyon, there had recently been another gifted prairie schoolmarm in the neighborhood, Georgia O'Keeffe, who taught school in Amarillo in 1912–1913; but Miss O'Keeffe went on to New York, Stieglitz, and glory, whereas Miss Debo merely trudged up to Washington and parked herself in the basement of the old Department of the Interior, where the records of the Dawes Commission were then kept.

This commission, which sat for twelve years (1893–1905), had the unenviable responsibility of making the Five Tribes—which had held their land communally, by treaty and patent—accept individual allotments of land and, also, the dissolution of their tribal governments, after which they would all be American citizens, resident in the new state of Oklahoma. The Five Tribes did not want, nor did they passively accept, the extinction of their titles and their sovereignty, but, as always, they were outnumbered, outlobbied, and outlawyered.

Angie Debo was, at first, anything but a breastbeater for Native American rights. Although she grew up on the edge of the Creek country, and was to write her finest book about the Creek people, I doubt that she had much to do with Indians or Indian affairs until she began her work on the Dawes Commission. She came from sodbuster stock, a breed, in my experience, that produces precious few sentimentalists. In the Choctaw book particularly, she is sometimes casually condescending to the Indians in the manner of her day (her contemporary, Samuel Eliot Morison, takes the same tone in his school history of the United States). But, as she plowed through the records in Washington and probed in rural courthouses back home, her sympathies shifted and her innate tough-mindedness began to be directed at the misdeeds of her own people (that is, white Oklahomans). She immediately perceived a major irony: American citizenship, dream and hope of millions of emigrants, was, for the real natives who were being forced to accept it, a tool of destruction. Citizenship was the legal crowbar which would be used to pry them off their land, since, once they were citizens, their land could be bought and sold like that of any other citizens.

Singularly, for a woman of her time and place, she recognized that the policy of allotments in which land that had once been tribal was surveyed and broken into section and quarter-section lots was, from the point of view of the Five Tribes, a tragedy that was at bottom religious in nature. Whatever their faults, the Indians (in the main) still held to a sacramental view of the earth as being holy and indivisible. The whites, whatever their virtues, didn't see it that way. For them, land was as salable as shoes, only it was worth more.

What the records of the Dawes Commission revealed to Angie Debo was, in the end, human nature—particularly human nature as it operated in eastern Oklahoma throughout the approach to statehood. What offended her most deeply at first were the broken promises: a sodbuster's word, after all, was his bond, and, to the plains pioneer, a promise made was a promise kept. Though her own parents had moved from Kansas to Oklahoma in search of more and better land, she had not expected to encounter such intense, obliterating land-greed as the records revealed. There was even, for a time, a *Dead Souls*-ish practice by which land speculators would buy up the allotments of Indians who had died but not yet been removed from the tribal rolls.

As she cut ever deeper into the story her respect for the bureaucrats diminished and her respect for the Indians grew, especially for leaders such as the wise Creek chieftain Pleasant Porter, who continued to act for his people with dignity during the whole confusing and humiliating business of apportionment. Many Indians, given allotments, never showed up to claim them. Some absentees acted out of principle, others out of resignation and hopelessness. One who dissented on principle was the Creek statesman Chitto Harjo, who once, in 1906, startled a senatorial committee by announcing bluntly: "Now I am going to tell you what has happened since 1492." The senators were aghast: Did the man suppose they had all day? Persuaded to condense his understanding of the treaty situation, Chitto Harjo—as quoted by Angie Debo—did so eloquently. Speaking of the whites that he had been taught to revere, he said:

> He told me that as long as the sun shines and the sky is up yonder these agreements will be kept.... He said as long as the sun rises it shall last; as long as the waters run it shall last; as long as the grass grows it shall last.... He said, "Just as long as you see the light here, just as long as you see this light glimmering over us, shall these agreements be kept, and not until all these things cease and pass away shall our agreement pass away"; that is what he said, and we believed it. We have kept every turn of that agreement. The grass is growing, the waters run, the sun shines, the light is with us, and the agreement is with us yet....

If our treaty writers had a collective failing it was a tendency to be swept by their own eloquence into purple depths of quasi-biblical prose. Offers of eternal possession were frequently, even casually, made, perhaps most embarrassingly with the Sioux, who were granted the Black Hills forever only to have them yanked back almost immediately when gold was discovered in them.

None of this is news, nor was it in the 1920s when Angie Debo began her work: greed-driven dispossession of the native people had long been a hemispheric habit; it continues in Amazonia to this hour. But ruin is particular, tragedy local. Her study of the intricate but ultimately brutal legal process that so demoralized the Five Tribes just prior to statehood turned Angie Debo from a provincial schoolteacher into an important historian. She wrote crudely in the beginning. Her training had given her method, but not polish. Only in her finest book, *The Road to Disappearance*, does the prose take cadence, the sentences become graceful. Though one is aware of this awkwardness in the early books, one forgives it, very much as one forgives Dreiser, and for the same reasons. Even when the sentences aren't smooth, they have sinew; the reader is pulled along by her strength of mind and power of sympathy.

Here, from *The Road to Disappearance*, are her descriptions of two ways of dealing with the vexing problem of capital murder. First, while the Creeks still had jurisdiction over their own criminals, there was the Creek way:

> The death penalty was inflicted with . . . gravity. The condemned always met his fate calmly and never failed to show a strong interest in the coffin purchased for him at public expense. A typical execution took place in Coweta district in 1879 when one Satanoke was shot for the murder of Foxtail. About two hundred and fifty persons had assembled. A religious service was conducted by Rev. James McHenry. Then Coweta Micco, the judge of the district, . . . made a speech pointing out the seriousness of murder and advising all to take warning. The prisoner next addressed the crowd and all came up and bade him goodbye. His wife and baby were then brought up; he took the child in his arms, prayed for its welfare, kissed it, and returned it to its mother. He next asked to see the coffin and "said it was a good coffin." The speechmaking and the informal reception following it lasted two hours, and the condemned man apparently

> took a solemn pleasure in the whole affair. He was then told to prepare himself for execution. He seated himself, removed his boots, and arranged his clothes. He asked the lighthorse captain what guns would be used, and a change was made from shotguns to rifles to suit his convenience...

When it was hanging day in Fort Smith, Arkansas, where Isaac Parker, the famous hanging judge, held court, red justice had been replaced with the redneck variety:

> ...The drunkenness and lawlessness of that wicked border town of Fort Smith was extremely demoralizing to the Indians that were called there as witnesses. The hanging furnished an occasion for a Roman holiday; the railroads ran special excursion trains, and coarse, morbid crowds filled the jail yard, laughing, cursing, fighting for points of vantage, until it was hard to clear a path for the condemned to walk to the gallows.

In both the Creek and Choctaw books she dutifully cobbles together the tribal histories, but clearly it is the end of these stories, not their remote beginnings, that really interests her. Dispossession is a strong theme—it was also her home story. Fortunately, she had both the technical ability and the breadth of mind to do it justice.

By the time her trilogy was completed and published, Angie Debo had more or less taken her leave of academia. She administered the Federal Writers Project in Oklahoma, co-edited the Oklahoma state guide, was a librarian for a while, taught occasionally, and did odd literary jobs. By 1943 she was calling herself a freelance writer; the thorough historian whose major texts rest firmly on thick pillars of footnotes began to attempt the sort of light work for which she was totally ill-suited. Three years after the Creek book she published a slight, quasi-fictional portrait of her hometown (or its equivalent) called *Prairie City*. Either the book or the prairie schoolmarm so beguiled Alfred Knopf that he conjured up something called the A. A. Knopf Fellowship in History and awarded it to her. It may be that they both thought she was going to become the new Mari Sandoz, the appealing Nebraska writer who, after years of struggle and rejection, finally saw *Old Jules* (1935), her biography of her pioneer father, become an immediate best-seller.

Prairie City was an awkward hybrid, part history, part sociology, part fiction, part memoir; not surprisingly, only the history worked. After spending twenty years acquiring a flexible historical prose, Angie Debo attempted to trade it in for something that might work in *Redbook*. This didn't succeed but, unfortunately, she was soon to do worse. The woman who had written so scathingly of Oklahoma boosterism and the progressivist rhetoric that had been used to justify the big land-grab from the Indians wrote a complacently boosterish history of Tulsa, and one of the state of Oklahoma itself that was not much better.

It is a pity that none of the fine WPA photographers who worked in Oklahoma during the dust bowl years thought to take a picture of her; if any did I haven't seen it. There are plenty of family photographs though, and these reveal her to have been a striking young woman. She was usually photographed with an enigmatic half-smile, a La Gioconda of the prairies; and the half-smile suggests something rather more forceful than mere high spirits. She was a notably attractive woman working in a place not exactly overripe with female beauty. One would suppose there were suitors, but, if so, none of them seems to have measured up, at least not long enough to secure a place in the record.

Among her odd jobs was a seminar in which she taught professionals who worked with Indian children, a task which led her to write her *History of the Indians of the United States*,[4] a wandering, sketchy

4. University of Oklahoma Press, 1970.

book that does her no credit—the subject, in any case, had grown so vast that the archaeological record alone would take a lifetime to master.

But, six years later, when she might have been expected to be an old prairie lady, fading out, she delivered the brilliant *Geronimo: The Man, His Time, His Place*,[5] a book she had been working on since at least the Fifties, when Jason Betzinez and one or two others who had been with Geronimo before he came in were still alive to be interviewed. The book is as persuasive a portrait of a nineteenth-century Indian leader as we are likely to have. The critical and analytical intelligence which Angie Debo had first applied over fifty years earlier to sort out the contradictions and inconsistencies in the treaty record, she now focused on the contradictions and inconsistencies in the several firsthand accounts of where Geronimo went or didn't, whom he killed or spared, and what he said or did when he was still a fighting Indian.

Her aim, she said, was to rescue Geronimo from being "just a Wild West character," a task ultimately beyond the power of any historian. The great characters of western history—Custer, Crazy Horse, Sitting Bull, Wild Bill Hickok, Billy the Kid, Geronimo—have long since risen out of history into myth. A permanent frustration for western historians, there almost from the beginning, is that, thanks largely to the movies, the lies about the West are more potent than the truths.

The trouble is that the great scenes are just so scriptable. Consider Geronimo's famous surrender, September 4, 1886, in Skeleton Canyon, near the Mexico–Arizona border. General Crook had just quit in disgust, having let Geronimo slip away again. The vainglorious Brigadier General Nelson A. Miles, the man who had been speedy enough, nearly a decade earlier, to head off the fleeing Nez Percé just south of

---

5. University of Oklahoma Press, 1976.

Canada, thus receiving (with General Howard) Chief Joseph's famous speech of surrender, is now just north of Mexico, with nearly a quarter of the United States Army somewhere in the Southwest, wondering if Geronimo will finally turn up and hoping he will be in a good mood if he does. Much as General Miles wants the glory of this last surrender, he is also afraid to believe in it; he knows full well that if Geronimo slips away again his portion will not be glory but disgrace—his and the army's as well. Finally, lured by the usual false promises, Geronimo allows the also very nervous Lieutenant Gatewood to ease him out of Mexico. When he at last surrenders to General Miles he has with him only Naiche (son of the Apache chief Cochise), sixteen warriors, fourteen women, and six children. He was not in a good mood, though, and made no immortal speech, though he did make a point he was to repeat over the years: that none of the generals or all of the armies had ever taken him in a fight. Or, as he put it, "never caught him shooting."

This strange event, the few Apaches, the many soldiers, the nervous general, the rocky canyon, the desert sun, occurred only four years before Angie Debo's birth; Geronimo lived in captivity for twenty-three years, dying at Fort Sill, Oklahoma, when she was a girl of nineteen. Chief Joseph was, by a little, the luckier man. He got to go back to his Idaho homeland once; Geronimo never saw the desert again.

Angie Debo takes us through Geronimo's life with the same discriminating judgment about sources that had distinguished her earlier work on the Choctaws and the Creeks. She has become a better narrative historian than she was when she was working on the Five Tribes, but the real singularity of *Geronimo* is that she manages—while remaining faithful to the history—to tell much of this celebrated story from the Apache, rather than the white, point of view. Almost all the movies and most of the books about Geronimo are really about what the white soldiers who were chasing him felt and did. They were about whites trying to subdue an unsubdued and entirely unrepentant native leader. Angie Debo's *Geronimo* is about the native leader himself, a man who eluded capture as long as he did because of his mastery of one of the most unforgiving landscapes in America; also, insofar as the historian can discern it, it is about what he felt as he saw his people's way of life ending, and the exceptionally determined fight he put up to delay this ending as long as possible. Angie Debo was not Apache, but she had learned, in her long life, how to listen to Indians. She did her best to grasp the mind-set of the desert Apache, and the result is a book that takes us as close as we will ever get to the period and the man.

With this her work was done, but, like Miss O'Keeffe, she didn't die. The Old Woman of the Desert and the Old Woman of the Steppe lived on and on, into the near shadow of a century, the one world-famous, the other occasionally getting asked to lead a rodeo parade. In her seventies, fearing that what had happened in Oklahoma was about to happen again in Alaska, she roused herself to lobby for the Native Claims Settlement Act. In her mid-nineties, she finally became cute. She bought herself a black bonnet and took to dressing like Queen Victoria, at least on state occasions. She also came to look and behave like her last great subject, Geronimo. Once finally caged in age, they both rattled their bars with a vengeance; both became shrewd managers of their own legends.

For myself, this short appreciation is a way of paying a little interest on a long-accruing debt. In 1950, when I was fourteen, I found a copy of *The Road to Disappearance* in the parking lot of a livestock auction in Wichita Falls, Texas. Oklahoma was only eight miles away; the book had probably fallen out of a pickup, sustained a direct hit by a cattle truck, and been clipped a time or two by horse-trailers. Even so, it was a book, and any book was manna to me then. Unfortunately I was with my father, not a man to simply drive off with somebody else's book, even if the true owner was by then hell-bound for Anadarko. He insisted that I take it to the auctioneer and tell him to put it in the lost and found. The auctioneer, so instructed, looked at me in astonishment: in the dog-eat-dog world of cattle auctions anything lost, if found, is likely to be immediately taken; and, besides, this was a *book* (an environment less conducive to reading than a livestock auction is hard to imagine). Still, he didn't want to cross my father, so he put the book on a shelf between a plug of chewing tobacco and about a hundred pencil stubs—he was a man who went through a lot of pencils.

Two weeks later, the book was still there, so I claimed it, rubbed off the tread marks as best I could, and took it home. I soon realized that I wasn't smart enough to read it—it was all about Creeks and treaties—but I put it on a shelf and considered it, dipping into it from time to time, reading a paragraph here and there, hoping I would someday be able to understand the whole, a process that took some forty years. My library at the time consisted of a few boys' books left me by a thoughtful cousin as he went away to World War II. I didn't know much, but I could tell that *The Road to Disappearance* was a different order of thing from *Poppy Ott and the Stuttering Parrot*, my favorite book up to then. What intrigued me about my new, slightly tread-marked volume was that it had evidently been written by a woman who lived in Oklahoma. Texans, like the Congress itself, were slow to accord Oklahoma the majesty of statehood; I thought of it as a region set aside for the unruly. My one Oklahoma uncle, when informed some years later that I was thinking of getting a Ph.D., seemed mildly surprised that I would think to mention such a thing to him: wasn't a Ph.D. just a posthole digger, an implement that could be obtained in any hardware store?

I didn't get the Ph.D, but I kept *The Road to Disappearance* and, by considering it and occasionally reading a few of Angie Debo's sinewy sentences, gradually arrived at a great notion, which was that it might be possible to organize one's life around literature—not write it, I didn't aspire to that, but just read it and, in some way, live with it.

The notion that one could organize one's life around literature might seem simple, but if you grow up where there are no books and where no writer is ever mentioned, it isn't. I could look off the porch of our ranch house, straight up the length of the Great Plains, all the way into Canada, but the only evidence I had that there were such things as writers in all that stretch of land was this book I had found in a parking lot, by a woman from Oklahoma. I didn't know about Willa Cather or Mari Sandoz; Gass and Woiwode had yet to peep above the grass of the Dakotas. And yet, a woman from Oklahoma had somehow ordered her life around books and study. Having that fact to contemplate was, in context, an inestimable gift.

Angie Debo's portrait now hangs in the Oklahoma state capitol. Among her companions there are Jim Thorpe, Will Rogers, and the great Sequoyah, whom she revered: all in all a fine honor for a prairie woman who had to struggle to get her schooling, but who, once she *had* the schooling, did something worthy of it.

Chapter 5

ZUNI

1.

How could any anthropologist with an iota of ambition possibly resist Zuni, an ancient, remote, impacted society, for centuries agrarian, with—I hope I get these numbers right—twelve matrilineal clans; thirteen medicine societies (sometimes called fraternities); the Koyemshi, or Mudheads (clown-priests); a society or group of highly trained masked dancers (male); a priesthood or theocracy of rainbringers (hereditary); and a much put-upon secular governor (elected) who has the thankless task of dealing with whatever non-Zunis might appear: soldiers from the nearby army base (Fort Wingate), missionaries of various faiths, tourists (usually lost), traders, speculators, looters, journalists, and, of course, those bloodsucking leeches the anthropologists themselves, one or more of whom have maintained a presence in or near Zuni almost continuously for one hundred and twenty years?

Add to this brutally oversimplified description a few witches, the occasional scatological rite, and a language that seems to bear no close relation to any other American Indian language, not even those of the twenty or so Pueblo societies that are comparatively nearby, and you have a siren song that has called many and called them far.

In the early 1970s it even called me, mainly because I read *Finding the Center*,[1] Dennis Tedlock's fine translations of Zuni narrative poetry —still the book that, in my opinion, takes one farther into the Zuni world than any other. Though I *found* Zuni easily enough, I could not figure out how to *arrive* there, in any way that seemed convincing, a feeling Eliza McFeely might sympathize with, since on the last page of her acute and engaging book, *Zuni and the American Imagination*,[2] she describes how she once drove right through Zuni, without actually realizing that she was there:

> You pass clusters of undistinguished buildings, and then, suddenly, right along the highway, which is a narrow two-lane road, there is a collection of tourist shops advertising Native American crafts, a gas station or two, a convenience store. Then, as suddenly, you are in open desert again, with scattered dwellings, a view of the distant mountains, and ahead of you is Arizona.
>
> Only when you retrace your steps, turning into the congested, narrow lanes to the south of the highway, do you discover the pueblo of your imagination. It is like an archaeological treasure buried beneath new buildings, hidden around corners of treacherously winding roads, quietly playing second fiddle to the beckoning marquee of the video store. Like their ancestors, who built that older town on the site of a still older one, . . . the Zunis have layered new forms onto old foundations, built the present upon the past.

This description of Zuni, which doesn't differ in many particulars

---

1. *Finding the Center: The Art of the Zuni Storyteller* (1972; University of Nebraska Press, second edition, 1989).

2. Hill and Wang, 2001.

from the one Edmund Wilson wrote when he went there in 1947,[3] puts a hopeful shine on a place that, to one less engrossed in the Zuni cosmos, might seem mainly bleak. I'm not sure that the great kachinas, who are supposed to order and balance the world, are happy to have the kivas of Zuni playing second fiddle to a video store.

Despite my admiration for *Finding the Center*, my problem may have been that I went to Zuni *without* having a pueblo in my imagination. I wasn't fishing for secrets, either; I even thought of carrying a sign saying "I Am Not an Anthropologist!" to diffuse suspicion. So closemouthed are the Zuni that just persuading someone to let me put gas in my car seemed like a major communications breakthrough; and yet, somehow, anthropologists have crowbarred their way into this deeply reserved society, one whose people are trained from birth not to reveal the sacred secrets, and made it yield a vast bibliography, hundreds of books and articles, ranging from the lightest tourist froth to the most dauntingly technical ethnology. If I had to characterize the Zuni or their Pueblo neighbors in one word the word would be "silent," and yet this silence has provoked a century-long chorus of anthropological voices: that's the paradox that forms the background for Eliza McFeely's short, smart book.

With fine insight and very welcome tact she describes how anthropology came to Zuni, her tact being the more welcome because it contrasts so sharply with the blazing rudeness of the first anthropologists to get there: Frank Cushing and Matilda Stevenson, two of the toughest customers ever to straddle a mule (though I suppose Mrs. Stevenson, a proper if by no means ordinary mid-Victorian, may have availed herself of a sidesaddle). They arrived in 1879. Zuni, to its frequent dismay, then became intellectual property which Frank and Matilda,

3. Edmund Wilson, *Red, Black, Blond, and Olive: Studies in Four Civilizations: Zuni, Haiti, Soviet Russia, Israel* (Oxford University Press, 1956).

who had come separately with her husband, fought over for twenty years. It may be that the only reason they got in at all was because the Zuni, for a few fatal seconds, couldn't believe that any two people could be so rude; in the pause Frank and Matilda kicked in the door, something they were not loath to do literally if they thought there was something inside that the young science of anthropology needed to know about.

2.

The youth of this new "science" should be stressed, not that it excuses the frequently patronizing behavior of the first scientists to attempt it. In 1877 Lewis Henry Morgan, long a student of the Iroquois and of Native American kinship systems, published *Ancient Society; or Researches in the Lines of Human Progress from Savagery through Barbarism to Civilization*, a book that excited Marx, Engels, and a number of other heavy thinkers. Morgan's evolutionary premise for social development is right there in the title; it was merely necessary for anthropologists to get out into the field and sketch in lines of progress as native societies everywhere rose inexorably toward the fully civilized condition.

In 1879, scarcely two years after Morgan's important book was published, John Wesley Powell—explorer, geologist, ethnologist, and bureaucrat—established the Bureau of American Ethnology. In the same year, aware that there was need for haste if valuable native vocabularies were to be saved, Powell dispatched his geologist colleague Colonel James Stevenson, Stevenson's anthropologist wife, Matilda, and a twenty-two-year-old clerk hastily borrowed from Spencer Baird's Smithsonian westward to the pueblos, whose mysterious antiquity he had noticed on his famous trips to the Grand Canyon. The borrowed clerk was Frank Hamilton Cushing, who in turn borrowed John Wesley

Powell's copy of Morgan's *Ancient Society*. The gifted photographer John Hillers completed the company—it is thanks to Hillers's camera that we can now have a visual sense of Zuni as it then was.

The Zunis, as I have said, had a secular governor, whose job it was to deal with outsiders. At the time of this little party's arrival at Zuni the governor was a man named Palowahtiwa, also called Patricio Pino in some texts. When Colonel Stevenson negotiated lodgings with Palowahtiwa for a brief stay, neither man supposed that a four-and-a-half-year occupation was about to begin. Frank Cushing was then living in a tent outside the village, with John Hillers. Dissatisfied, fearing, perhaps, that Matilda Stevenson might scoop him, or, at the very least, loot before he could loot—the Stevensons, over their years of travel in the West, were said to have sent back as many as 33,000 artifacts—Cushing, one day, simply took his hammock and hung it in Palowahtiwa's house. All concerned—Palowahtiwa, his grandmother, numerous Zunis, the Stevensons, etc.—were horrified, but Frank Cushing defied them all. He simply wouldn't leave. The Stevensons couldn't compel him and the Zunis couldn't dislodge him. Though Cushing made trips here and there, usually to seek out sacred caves or other sites the Zunis particularly didn't want him to see, his hammock stayed more or less put for four and a half years. He had left a fiancée in the East; in time he married her and brought her to Zuni, along with her sister. His wife, Emily Cushing, a forceful young woman, soon introduced to Zuni the quaint custom of knocking before entering, a formality the Zuni had previously seen no great need for.

From Frank Cushing's chutzpah an anthropological method was born: many hundreds of field-workers have since hung their hammocks in places where they were not wanted; but for Cushing the hammock was only the beginning. As soon as he gained a little foothold in the language he began to butt in constantly, plopping himself down at religious councils in the kivas and elsewhere. Again, the Zunis failed to dislodge him. Many would no doubt have preferred merely to knock him in the head, but Zuni experience of white power had been long and unpleasant—Coronado had trampled through Zuni in 1540, and there had been periods of sharp conflict since. Fort Wingate was not far away—putting up with the young upstart was better than risking trouble with the soldiers, though the soldiers soon had their own problems with Cushing, particularly after the Zunis made him a member of the prestigious Priesthood of the Bow. He then began to style himself First Warchief of Zuni and was soon taking potshots at Navajo horses if he saw them grazing on Zuni land. One mule, borrowed, returned, not returned, lost, not lost, troubled relations with the military for a considerable time.

Cushing, once settled in Palowahtiwa's house, soon adopted a faux Zuni costume. The admiring and aspiring young Dutch anthropologist Herman Ten Kate, meeting Cushing at Zuni after the latter had been there some years, described Cushing's outfit as "half Indian, half fantasy"; there are those who would argue that "half Indian, half fantasy" might do as a description of Cushing's anthropology as well. Eliza McFeely notes that Cushing had absolute confidence in his ethnological intuition where Zuni history, prehistory, and ceremonial were concerned. If he couldn't establish something archaeologically, or by recourse to informants, he was not loath to allow his own imagination to plaster in the gaps; after all, who except Matilda Stevenson would be likely to dispute him? That lady had scribbled *her* opinion of him on the back of a picture of Cushing in native garb:

> Frank Hamilton Cushing in his fantastic dress worn while among the Zuni Indians. The man was the biggest fool and charlatan I ever knew. He even put his hair up in curl papers every night. How could a man walk weighted down with such toggery?

What Cushing was doing in donning such toggery was the same thing that his near contemporaries Buffalo Bill and Theodore Roosevelt were doing at almost the same time: using costume, showmanship, and the popular press to enhance their professional activities. "My Adventures in Zuni," Cushing's series of popular articles, appeared in *The Century Illustrated Monthly Magazine* in 1882 and 1883; his more technical anthropology dribbled out at a slow trickle, and his summa, *Zuni Breadstuff*, did not appear in book form until twenty years after his death.

Without Frank Cushing's showmanship and flair for publicity—which should not obscure the fact that life at Zuni in the 1880s involved some real hardship—it is doubtful that Zuni could ever have been squeezed into the already overstuffed shopping bag of the American imagination; and, even so, as Eliza McFeely acknowledges, it's been an in-and-out sort of thing, the Zuni of today being less famous than the Zuni of one hundred years ago. But there *has* been a parade of sorts: the anthropologist Elsie Clews Parsons (usually newsworthy because of her money and her feminism) went there, Ruth Benedict went there (at the same time as the less heralded Ruth Bunzel), Edmund Wilson went there, Aldous Huxley had a Zuni-like place in *Brave New World*, ditto Robert Heinlein in *Stranger in a Strange Land*, and America, like a sleepy dog, opens one eye and tries to focus on Zuni for a few minutes before resuming its slumbers. Frank Cushing in his fantasy outfit, trumpeting to the world that he was First Warchief of Zuni, at least got some attention, both for Zuni and for anthropology itself.

How Cushing came to be made a Bow Priest is a story with a few odd twists. In the early 1970s the anthropologist Triloki Nath Pandey, of St. John's College, Cambridge, produced a fascinating article on Zuni responses to the various anthropologists who had trooped through. In the article Pandey reveals that Cushing was not the first white man to be offered membership in this priesthood: the first was a prominent southwesterner named Albert Banta, who declined the honor. What that suggests is that the Zuni were really looking for a lobbyist, and they got an exceptionally good one in Frank Cushing. Probably one of the reasons he was recalled to Washington was that he successfully defended the Zunis' right to a particular spring against the efforts of a powerful senator, whose son wanted to start a ranch where the spring was.

Awkwardly for Frank Cushing, candidates for the Bow Priesthood were required to present a scalp, presumably one taken in a warrior-like engagement. Cushing secured two scalps from collections in the East but was bluntly told that that wouldn't cut it. Then some Apaches pulled off a raid, after which Cushing showed up with a somewhat fresher hank of hair. It's hard to imagine an Apache dimwitted enough to let Frank Cushing kill him, even if Cushing would have gone that far, which I don't believe. His letters and field reports, well edited by Jesse Green as *Cushing at Zuni*,[4] reveal him to be boastful, cunning, superior in a Curzon-like way, and highly political, but they hardly suggest a killer of men. Possibly he dug up a Navajo and took his scalp.

Cushing has sometimes been criticized for having guessed too much, and for playing fast and loose with artifacts; the notion that tribal objects should be studied in their social context was still far in the future. On the other hand he has respectable advocates, Edmund Wilson for one. Wilson thought Cushing's collection of Zuni folktales able to stand comparison with Joel Chandler Harris's Uncle Remus stories. More of a puzzler, to me at least, is Wilson's contention that Cushing's writing rather resembles that of C. M. Doughty, of *Arabia Deserta* fame. Maybe Wilson was thinking of the quasi-biblical dialogue both men were prone to. Here's Cushing, from the *Zuni Folk Tales*:

> But the old Deer-mother said to him: "Hush, my child! Thou art but a mortal, and though thou might'st live on the roots of the trees and the bushes and plants that mature in autumn, yet surely in the winter time thou could'st not live, for my supply of

4. *Cushing at Zuni: The Correspondence and Journals of Frank Hamilton Cushing 1879–1884*, edited by Jesse Green (University of New Mexico Press, 1990).

> milk will be withholden, and the fruits and the nuts will all be gone. . . ."

And Doughty, from somewhere near the House of Fools:

> "Out!" cried the savage wretch, in that leaping up and laying hold upon my mantle. . . . "Dost thou not know me yet? . . . *Ya rubbâ*, O fellowship, ye are witnesses of this man's misdoing. . . ."

Claude Lévi-Strauss said Cushing deserved to sit at the right hand of Lewis Henry Morgan, another puzzler. Could Lévi-Strauss have seen in some of Cushing's reports the beginnings of a structural approach to social classification? Or did the man who wrote, in the first paragraph of his most popular book, *Tristes Tropiques*, "Anthropology is a profession in which adventure plays no part, . . ." actually admire Cushing for having hung that hammock? After all, the French master hung quite a few himself, before scraping off what he calls the "fungus" of adventure.

It is worth repeating that Frank Cushing didn't hang his hammock in just any old house. He hung it in the house of the governor. Practically everything Cushing did irritated Matilda Stevenson, but this move must have particularly infuriated her, since it preempted her own access to the powerful Pino family.

When Cushing finally left Zuni, Matilda Stevenson came back and secured an important informant of her own, We'wha, the tallest person in Zuni. We'wha accompanied the Stevensons to Washington, where, as the "Zuni Princess," she met President Cleveland, gave weaving demonstrations, and was the hit of the social season in 1885. We'wha was in fact a male transvestite, a berdache, having chosen at puberty to wear women's clothes and do women's work, a quite acceptable choice in Zuni society. We'wha paid close attention to the ways of the capital and was able to report when he got home that most of the white women were frauds: he had been in the ladies' rooms with them and seen them remove their false teeth and take "rats" out of their hair.

But the friendship with Matilda Stevenson seems to have been genuine. When Mrs. Stevenson was at last confronted with the fact that her old friend was, biologically at least, a male, she responded touchingly:

> As the writer could never think of her faithful and devoted friend in any other light, she will continue to use the feminine gender when referring to We'wha....

Eliza McFeely follows Mrs. Stevenson's practice in regard to gender; Will Roscoe, whose excellent biography of We'wha, *The Zuni Man-Woman*, appeared in 1991, uses "he."

In 1904 Matilda Stevenson published her long report, *The Zuni Indians: Their Mythology, Esoteric Fraternities and Ceremonies*. As Eliza McFeely notes, it was a kind of encyclopedia of all things Zuni; her rival Frank Cushing never saw it. Four years earlier he had choked on a bone and was dead at the dinner table, aged forty-three. Mrs. Stevenson would have been delighted could she have known about an incident reported by Triloki Nath Pandey:

> You see, the Zuni are a funny people. They always complain that whatever anthropologists have written about them is a pack of lies. But I can tell you that many times old Zuni priests have come to this place [the trading store] and have waited for hours before everyone had left. Then, they would come to me and say, "Can I see Stevenson's book? We want to have a dance and I want to see how the dancers look in her pictures."[5]

5. Triloki Nath Pandey, "Anthropologists at Zuni," *Proceedings of the American Philosophical Society*, Vol. 116, No. 4 (August 15, 1972), p. 329.

3.

The third person mentioned by Eliza McFeely as having helped to establish Zuni in the American imagination is the curator Stewart Culin, of what is now the Brooklyn Museum. Culin had a genius for mounting exhibitions, Indian exhibitions particularly; one reason he is in this book is that Eliza McFeely, as she freely admits, can't resist Indian exhibits. Culin bought aggressively at a time when there was plenty to choose from. He went into the field occasionally but preferred to buy from traders—between Culin, Cushing, and the Stevensons it's a wonder there's a pot left west of the Rio Grande. Culin's exhibitions to an extent memorialized Frank Cushing's career. He even wore Cushing's faux Zuni outfit to a dinner in his honor at the Salmagundi Club.

Frank Cushing died, Matilda Stevenson published her big book, Stewart Culin mounted his striking exhibitions; and, soon enough, before the twentieth century was even a decade old, a new generation of anthropologists was underfoot at Zuni. If one allows for a bit of elasticity in the definition of a generation these would include Franz Boas (there for a few days), A. L. Kroeber, Leslie Spier, Elsie Clews Parsons, Ruth Bunzel, Ruth Benedict, and a host of others. Anthropological emphasis had shifted decisively away from Morgan, and his conviction of progress, toward a cultural relativism that saw native cultures as individual, discrete, many-patterned; and anthropology, whether discipline, profession, or science, now firmly separated itself from belles lettres. The number of books that could be read for pleasure by nonspecialists were few, and these few, such as Margaret Mead's famous *Coming of Age in Samoa*, were usually attacked as bad anthropology.

Ruth Benedict's *Patterns of Culture*, a relativist treatment of three cultures, attracted considerable attention when it appeared in 1934. Zuni was one of the cultures; Benedict had been there a decade earlier, for a time sharing a room with Ruth Bunzel, who worked out a

Zuni grammar and also classified the kachinas. Benedict took an old Nietzschean label—Apollonian—and slapped it on Zuni; it suggests that Zuni society is moderate, cautious, consensus-seeking, structured so as to discourage any Dionysian impulse toward excessive individualism: more or less the qualities one might expect a none too populous people, living in an arid place, with little arable land and less water, to encourage. It is also congruent with the Zuni's belief that they live in the Middle Place, a place they have ascended to from depth and darkness, guided by the twins, the Ahayuuta, brothers formed of foam and by the sun.

Still, it's possible to suspect that these Apollonian characteristics provide less than a full picture of Zuni. Apollonianism doesn't save the occasional witch or sorcerer, or prevent century-long feuds. Try to explain to their neighbors the Navajo that the Zuni are moderates and you'll probably get a big laugh. The characterization may reflect a time when the Zunis were more cohesive than any people can be once the video store sets up next door to the church.

The more famous an anthropologist becomes, the greater the likelihood that he or she will be accused of completely mischaracterizing the people they became famous for characterizing in the first place. This has just happened to Napoleon Chagnon, who, Patrick Tierney tells us in *Darkness in El Dorado*, first called the Yanomamo "the fierce people." Eliza McFeely suggests that anthropology has the capacity to work like a mirror, ". . . reflecting back the cultural certainties and uncertainties of the anthropologists themselves." So must we now consider the Yanomamo gentle and Napoleon Chagnon fierce? And what aspect of ourselves do we see when we consider, as she has, our century-long stare at Zuni? American relentlessness grinding through Zuni resistance?

Edmund Wilson, at Zuni in 1947, was so impressed by the great Sha'lako dancers, with their ten-foot-high masks and their extraordinary abilities as dancers, that he compared them to the Ballets Russes.

Though Wilson behaved pretty well while at Zuni, leaving places when he was told to leave—something neither Frank Cushing nor Matilda Stevenson could be bothered to do with any frequency—he still had some trouble as he made his way back to his lodgings, after the dance. Zuni had no streetlights or, in the strict sense, even any streets. While floundering around in the darkness Wilson fell into a pit and, later, was bitten by "hyena-like" dogs. Probably a witch put that pit in Edmund Wilson's way, to remind him that he wasn't necessarily welcome in the Middle Place.

The dogs, I imagine, were acting on their own.

Chapter 6

COOKIE PIONEERS

Patricia Nelson Limerick began her admirable career as a student of ghost towns, those dusty, blistered counterstatements to the triumphalist version of the winning of the American West. If we won the West so decisively, how come there are so many ghost towns, places where pioneer hopes seem to have been totally defeated? (In my own small county in Texas three communities have vanished utterly, not a chimney, not a brick, not a log to remind of us of the ambitions that once had been nourished there.)

That question writ large—what about the failures (commercial, environmental, cultural, administrative, familial, moral) that accompanied the winning of the West?—animates Ms. Limerick's important first book, *The Legacy of Conquest* (1987), which is filled with counterstatements to the triumphalist narrative. She is, perhaps by instinct, a counterstater, even, on occasion, a counterpuncher, as in this little rat-a-tat-tat to the chin of Henry James:

> We live on haunted land, on land that is layers deep in human passion and memory. There is, today, no longer any point in sorting out these passions and memories into starkly separate forms of ownership. Whether the majority who died in any particular site were Indians or whites, these places literally ground

> Americans of all backgrounds in their common history. In truth, the tragedies of the wars are our national joint property, and how we handle that property is one test of our unity or disunity, maturity or immaturity, as a people wearing the label "American."
>
> For a century or two, white American intellectuals labored under the notion that the United States was sadly disadvantaged when it came to the joint property of history. The novelist Henry James gave this conviction of American cultural inferiority its most memorable statement: "The past, which died so young and had time to produce so little, attracts but scanty attention." "The light of the sun seems fresh and innocent," James wrote, "as if it knew as yet but few of the secrets of the world and none of the weariness of shining."
>
> The sun that shines on North America has, it turns out, seen plenty. A claim of innocence denies the meaning of the lives of those who died violently in the conquest of this continent, and that denial diminishes our souls.

Souls don't show up too often in American historiography nowadays; they don't show up very often in Ms. Limerick's work, either, only being mentioned when she feels that American experience is being condescended to. Usually she's temperate, even good-natured, though of course always on the alert for mixed messages and other forms of confusion:

> Let me call your attention as an example of the drawing of historical lessons to a quite extraordinary book, published in 1993, by Emmett C. Murphy with Michael Snell, called *The Genius of Sitting Bull: 13 Heroic Strategies for Today's Business Leader*. This book takes stories from Sitting Bull's life and draws from them applications for today's business world. Here are the basic terms of the analogy:

> The historical Battle of the Little Bighorn took place on June 25, 1876. It represented the most ignominious defeat ever suffered by American armed forces. Today, more than 100 years later, America's economic and social forces have come dangerously close to a similar humiliation.

> Does this make sense? If it was Sitting Bull who inflicted that ignominious defeat in 1876, would not the application of Sitting Bull's strategies serve the goal of defeating the United States once again? This apparent contradiction does not trouble the authors, nor should it. It is a fundamental aspect of the romanticizing of Western history, that you simply dissolve context and encounter Sitting Bull, not as a person engaged in serious warfare against the United States but as an abstract, courageous, inspirational figure from the colorful Western past. . . .

What Ms. Limerick is dealing with here is a clumsiness, not a contradiction. The authors appear to be laboring to say that, bygones being bygones, Sitting Bull's strategies can now be put to work for us, rather than against us, though, as I read the literature of the Little Bighorn, the main manifestation of his genius in relation to *that* battle was that he predicted it, in the great dance-trance he achieved about a week before the battle, in which he saw soldiers falling into camp; and lo, through the (in this case negative) genius of Custer they *did* fall into camp—they fell forever, as it turned out.

But the larger point Ms. Limerick makes in the passage quoted above, that the dissolving of context is fundamental to the romanticizing of the West, is valid and important. It has been Ms. Limerick's task—and that of her revisionist colleagues—to continually restore the contexts which the romanticizers just as continually dissolve. She is, I'm afraid, the Historian as Sisyphus, endlessly rolling the rock of realism up Pike's Peak, only to watch it roll right back down into the pines of romance. Hers—theirs—is a noble but thankless task; rain though they may on the rodeo-parade model of western history, it's still that parade that people line up to see: there'll be an Indian or two, if any can be located, and a couple of faux Conestoga wagons, maybe a stagecoach, with a tottery old-timer riding shotgun, then a riding club, with a number of bankers and businessmen nervously clutching their saddlehorns, and, finally, several Cadillac convertibles with pretty girls in them. There you have the beloved story: wagons rolling on across the wide Missouri, then Roy Rogers and Gene Autry, then Cadillacs (or, more currently, sport utility vehicles) whizzing along I-90, I-80, I-70, and so on down the ladder of roads.

Still, there are in the history departments gifted dog soldiers who insist on a different narrative. Patricia Nelson Limerick is one of their leaders; in *their* narrative, instead of an orderly parade, the winning of the West comes in a series of lurches, such as a car makes when it isn't running too well. There was a lurch to the fur country, to a gold strike or a silver lode, to an oil field, or, perhaps most typically, just a lurch away from what lay behind, something rather like the famous defiant lurch at the end of *Thelma and Louise*, the one that took the travelers right off a cliff.

The revisionist narrative may be tolerated nowadays but it is not welcomed, much less loved, in part, I suspect, because too many westerners have too much built-in ambivalence about their own experience. Even the Master (that's Louis L'Amour, not Henry James, please) had a little ambivalence. Ms. Limerick reports:

> ...L'Amour is the mid-twentieth century's successor to Zane Grey, a writer still intoxicated with the independence, nobility, grandeur, and adventure of the frontier. He remains true to the plot formula of tough men in a tough land. "A century ago," L'Amour wrote in a commentary in 1984, "the Western plains were overrun by buffalo, and many a tear has been shed

> over their passing, but where they grazed we now raise grain to feed a large part of the world...." This process of progress through conquest reached no terminus: "We are a people born to the frontier, and it has not passed. Our move into space opened the greatest frontier of all, the frontier that has no end."
>
> But only a year later, in 1985, circumstances disclosed a different Louis L'Amour. "Louis L'Amour's Real Life Showdown," the headline in the *Denver Post* read, "Western Author, Colorado Ute Duel Over Proposed Power-Line." L'Amour's idyllic ranch in southwest Colorado faced the threat of "a 345,000-volt power line," which would frame his view of the mountains...and which might trigger "health problems, ranging from headaches and fatigue to birth defects and cancer." L'Amour fought back with the conventional Western American weapon—the lawsuit—not the six-gun.
>
> If L'Amour recognized the irony in his situation, he did not share it with reporters. The processes of Western development do run continuously from past to present, from mining, cattle raising, and farming to hydroelectric power and even into space. The power line is a logical outcome of the process of development L'Amour's novels celebrate. But in this particular case the author was facing the costs of development, of conquest, and not simply cheering for the benefits. "People never worry about these things until it's too late," L'Amour said.... Eighty-eight books later, he was at last hot on the trail of the meanings of Western history.

I feel sure that one reason for the immense, continuing popularity of Louis L'Amour's works is that he shared no ironies; conversely, the fact that Ms. Limerick's works are so heavily laced with irony explains much of the resentment they engender in the West, where a love-it-or-leave-it attitude is not uncommon. Irony is thought to be an agent of disillusion and thus, unpatriotic; the mayors and the poetasters won't touch it.

Despite this, Patricia Nelson Limerick must be one of the most contented academics on the planet. She seems to love university life, love professors, and she holds forth vigorously and fearlessly from a well-defended redoubt at the University of Colorado. In the acknowledgments to *Something in the Soil*[1] she thanks nearly two hundred people, the majority of them professors. This is a lot more gratitude than usually gets heaped on the professorial caste.

She did her graduate work at Yale, sipping early from the fount of revisionism. Also, while in New Haven, she seems to have slipped across campus in order to pick up a few things at the Deconstruction Store; quite the most brilliant historical set piece in *Something in the Soil* is her elegant deconstruction of the weird, sad, unnecessary Modoc War in northern California in 1872–1873, a war Ms. Limerick breaks into twelve possible narrative lines leading to a like number of morals. Here is her opinion about the barriers to simple narrative lines where American events are concerned:

> If you place yourself at a certain distance, there is no clearer fact in American history than the fact of conquest. In North America, just as in much of South America, Africa, Asia, and Australia, Europeans invaded a land fully occupied by natives. Sometimes by negotiation and sometimes by warfare the natives lost ground and the invaders gained it. From the caves in the lava beds of northern California, where the Modocs held off the United States Army for months, to the site along the Mystic River in Connecticut, where Puritans burned Pequots trapped in a stockade, the landscape bears witness to the violent subordination of

---

1. Norton, 2000.

> Indian people. These haunted locations are not distant, exotic sights set apart from the turf of our normal lives.
>
> And yet distance makes these facts deceptively clear. Immerse yourself in the story of the dispossession of any one group, and clarity dissolves. There is nothing linear or direct in these stories. Only in rare circumstances were the affairs that we call "white–Indian wars" only matters of whites against Indians. More often, Indians took part on both sides, tribe against tribe or faction against faction....
>
> Moreover, if Indians were often divided against each other the same shortage of solidarity applied to the other side.... In virtually every case, the story of how the war got started and how it proceeded is a long, detailed, and tangled business. These are narratives designed to break the self-esteem of storytellers. You can be the world's greatest enthusiast for narrative history, and you can still lose your nerve at the prospect of putting yourself at the mercy of these tales from hell....

Ms. Limerick is fortunate in being able to remember the exact date on which she had her determinative insight about the West: that its problems were the legacy of conquest. The insight came in June of 1981, while she was at a conference in Sun Valley. While perhaps not so resonant as Gibbon's intimation of the *Decline and Fall*, which came while he was sitting in the ruins of the Capitol, listening to the barefoot friars singing vespers, Ms. Limerick's moment of vision did come in Sun Valley, itself certainly a legacy of conquest, and an ever more significant one, now that the New York investment banker Herbert Allen has started convening his annual conference of zillionaires nearby.

Henry James grew tired of having to talk about *Daisy Miller*, Bing Crosby got enough of having to sing "White Christmas," and it is likely that Patricia Nelson Limerick will one day grow weary of the phrase "legacy of conquest," although it represents, for her, a kind of historical true north. It seems to have evolved from a most incautious remark of Thomas Jefferson's:

> If there be one principle more deeply rooted than any other in the mind of every American, it is that we should have nothing to do with conquest.

Jefferson wrote that in 1791, in a letter to William Short; a little more than a decade later Lewis and Clark were on their way.

Were it not that Ms. Limerick is fastidious about titles, and constantly conscious of the need to write well—she even throws in a few pages of writing tips for the benefit of students and colleagues—she could simply have called her new book *The Legacy of Conquest II*; the new book is a grab bag of studies and reflections, most of which extend or amplify themes initiated in her earlier study.

In *Something in the Soil* she considers the Modoc War, Mormonism, Chinese- and Japanese-Americans, California, environmentalism, and the image of the American West as it appears in textbooks. In mid-book she takes leave, for a time, of the new history (about women, minorities, and the environment), goes back to the old history (about powerful white men), and gives us interesting reconsiderations of three such men: Juan Bautista de Anza (Spanish explorer, for a time in the eighteenth century governor of New Mexico), John Sutter (northern California land baron and self-invented overreacher), and Frederick Jackson Turner (the professor who, for simplicity's sake, we might just call the father of frontier studies). After the essay on the Modoc War I liked the chapter on Sutter best, perhaps because of a weakness for self-invented overreachers.

At one point Ms. Limerick even lets her hair down and admits that she cried a lot during the 1960s, an admission which allows her to devote a few pages to the New Emotionalism (my caps).

Ms. Limerick lopes over a vast territory in these studies; there are no doubt scholars who will fight her for every acre of it. One advantage she has in scholarly sparrings is that she writes very well. The cover copy for *The Legacy of Conquest* informs us that she contributes regularly to *USA Today*, making her that rare thing in our culture, a public historian, one who could easily, with a little effort, work her way up to the Talk of the Town:

> American undergraduates are . . . inclined to the breezy and colorful school of ethnicity and culture. Twenty years ago, a curious habit of mind seemed to take over the students. Repeatedly, in midterm and final exams, they would refer to various lifestyles, to the lifestyle of the Pequot or the lifestyle of the Puritans. It did not help me, in my adjustment to the students' fondness for this word, to hear a repeated radio announcement for a furniture store. The store claimed to offer every kind of furniture you might want, whether, as the ad said, "your lifestyle is colonial or contemporary." It is a wonderful and wild notion to think of someone in the late twentieth century choosing to have a colonial lifestyle, with a few stools, no chairs, a milk churn, a fireplace to cook in, a few pots, and, if privileged, a spoon or two, with life punctuated by an occasional raid or war of conquest, and with a general sense of subordination to a distant empire.

Then there's her approach to John Sutter:

> "Men! They never change"—that is one viable interpretation of the meaning of John Sutter for our times. Sutter is often referred to as the "Father of California." If Sutter did not, in literal fact, father California, that failure cannot be blamed on any lack of trying. With his Hawaiian mistress and his many encounters

> with Indian women and with Indian girls, ... in these matters of personal behavior, behavior dampened but not ended by the arrival of the wife he had abandoned in Switzerland in 1834, Sutter seems distinctly modern.

It is also fun to follow Ms. Limerick as she tracks such fundamental concepts as "frontier" or "pioneer" through the headlines of the past few decades. Here's a much abbreviated list, from her vast collection of contemporary references to pioneers:

> Cookie Pioneer
> Two Cinnamon Roll Pioneers
> Pioneer of Edible Landscapes
> Pioneer of Microwave Popcorn
> Peekaboo Pioneer (Frederick's of Hollywood)

Though Ms. Limerick has done much good work in this line, the West is a big place and many opportunities remain. I'll mention only two, both of which need to be sprinkled with a little scholarly gold dust. Since Ms. Limerick likes to deconstruct textbooks, in order to see how the West is faring from decade to decade, she can hardly afford to neglect the weirdest western textbook ever published, *Texas History Movies*,[2] a history text in comic-strip form. *The Texas Monthly* called *Texas History Movies* the second most influential Texas book of the twentieth century, after *Lonesome Dove*, but the ranking is clearly wrong. My novel may have lent its name to a few subdivisions (Dove Estates), forty or fifty saloons, and a lot of horses, but *Texas History Movies*, at times an officially sanctioned vehicle of historical instruction, stopped two generations of Texas public school

2. Text by John Rosenfield Jr., illustrations by Jack Patton (Dallas: The Southwest Press, 1928).

students dead in their tracks where history is concerned. The brainchild of a Dallas newspaperman, funded initially by an oil company, first issued in the mid-Twenties, *Texas History Movies* was still very much around my high school in the early Fifties, as a bootleg but widely used text. The effect, not to mention the irreverence, of those comics would be hard to overstate. When I reached a university I was shocked to discover that history was supposed to be learned from wordy books with few pictures and no comics; to this day I can't shake the conviction that Sam Houston, Santa Anna, and other luminaries of Lone Star history must have looked just as they appeared in *Texas History Movies*.[3]

The second development that needs investigating is the rise of the Empire of Valet Park, in Los Angeles. Woody Allen's old mot—that southern California's one contribution to civilization is the right to turn right on red—needs a hasty update. Now there's another contribution, the system of Valet Park, which insures that the person who drives the automobile will not be the person who parks it, particularly if the parking is to take place in one of the tonier zip codes such as Beverly Hills 90210. I first developed a slight sense of menace in relation to Valet Park a year or two ago, when I stopped to drop off some laundry and watched helplessly as my car was whisked away. Later, when I went back to pick up my clothes and looked at the bill I decided that the notion must be that I would just give them my car as a down payment on the cleaning.

There's a legacy of conquest for you, Valet Park. Ms. Limerick, sharp of eye and quick of retort, should get on it. It would make a dandy story for *USA Today*.

---

3. In 1974 the Texas State Historical Association and the Texas Educational Association published a new, much abbreviated edition, with an introduction by George B. Ward. It omits a number of cartoons in order to remove ethnic slurs and revises the text to correct "historical inaccuracies." The book is currently available through the Historical Association.

Chapter 7

POWELL OF THE COLORADO

Donald Worster has devoted most of an impressive career to writing about American water—or the lack of it. His book *Dust Bowl* (1979) is still the best study of that catastrophe; his *Rivers of Empire* (1985) offers a somber but solid assessment of what water management—or, rather, mismanagement—has done to the West. He concludes, correctly, that the Colorado River has essentially died as a part of nature, to be reborn as money. The Colorado may be the most exploited river in the West, but it is not the only one. Much of the fabled Missouri, river of Lewis and Clark, has been impounded too.

Professor Worster has now gone to the headwaters of American riverine policy in *A River Running West: The Life of John Wesley Powell*, a large biography of the one-armed geologist who twice ran the Grand Canyon of the Colorado River and lived to fight long and difficult bureaucratic battles in his efforts to promote a sane water policy for the arid lands of America. One hundred and thirty years of continuous litigation over water rights, with no end in sight, suggests that Powell didn't succeed.

An awkwardness Professor Worster tries to deal with right up front is that Wallace Stegner—one of Donald Worster's strongest advocates

---

1. Oxford University Press, 2001.

—happens to have written an especially brilliant book about Major Powell. It's called *Beyond the Hundredth Meridian* (1954); here are Donald Worster's reasons for trying to go beyond it:

> Stegner's book now ranks as one of the most influential books ever written about the West, and more than any other work its publication explains Powell's resurrection to sainthood after World War Two. Yet Stegner's biography was based on limited research into its subject or the nation's development. And it laid such strong claim to Powell as a Man of the West, a prophet for the arid region, that it obscured the fact that he was, above all, an intensely nationalistic American.

There's no reason at all why Donald Worster shouldn't write a book about John Wesley Powell, and he's written a good book; but if he is trying to pump himself for the task by picking chinks out of Stegner's book, he's chosen the wrong chinks. *Beyond the Hundredth Meridian* carries seventy pages of intelligent notes on Stegner's research, and the notion that Worster's Powell is somehow more "nationalistic" than Stegner's Powell is hard to credit. Both Stegner and Worster keep Powell in the West as long as possible, because that's where the portrait gets its color. Both men know that Powell and his wife, Emma, moved into a house on M Street in Washington, D.C., in 1872, and that Powell spent the rest of his working life as a bureaucrat. And, as writers, both Stegner and Worster know that long rehashes of a one-hundred-thirty-year-old bureaucratic battle are not likely to pull many readers to the edge of their seats.

John Wesley Powell *was* a man of vision—we'll get to that—but, as a bureaucrat, what he could never ignore was the necessity of getting funded. He won some battles, he lost some battles, he tied some battles, but he was never free of the struggle to secure adequate appropriations. When in 1890 his enemies, led by Senator William Stewart of Nevada, the so-called Silver Senator, finally defeated his well-thought-out plan for land classification and irrigation studies in the arid region, they beat him by cutting off his money. Indeed, until late in his career, when his two fiefdoms, the Geological Survey and the Bureau of Ethnology, were on secure footings, Powell could never relax about money. His first trips west in the 1860s, to collect specimens and artifacts for a tiny natural history museum he had helped create at Illinois State Normal University, would not have been possible had he not managed to persuade General Grant, his old commander, to allow his party to secure food cheaply from army posts. One lesson he learned thoroughly during his long years in Washington was that the canyons of the US Congress were no less perilous than the canyons of the Colorado had been.

Wallace Stegner did say, on the first page of *Beyond the Hundredth Meridian*, that he wasn't interested in Major Powell's personality, but he could hardly have written 438 pages about Powell's achievement without giving some glimpses into the personality that produced the achievement. Donald Worster has now supplied much of the biographical material that Wallace Stegner chose to avoid. That Worster might have been wise to skimp on family matters himself is attested to by this rather hangdog effort to say *something* about Powell's marriage to Emma:

> How the Powells managed domestic life is hard to determine in detail. Emma, it is clear, ran the place as a stay-at-home housewife, though her maternal responsibilities remained small. They had only the one child, Mary, who grew to adulthood in this house. Why there were no more children must be left to mere guesswork—was it due to infertility or incompatibility? How Emma passed her days, year following year, is also a mystery. She had charge of the budget for clothes and furnishings. She had friends who regularly came for tea and conversation, but it is beyond knowing what they talked about or whether the Major joined them in a laughing circle or retreated to his office.

That way lies tedium. Both Stegner and Worster know that there's only so far one can go with Major Powell as a personality. He sat in many public hearings, he worked closely with a number of fellow geologists—Clarence Dutton, Karl Gilbert, and the bon vivant Clarence King for three—but it is not evident that anyone thought he was easy to know, though all would have agreed that he was intensely ambitious. When editors finally got their hands on the manuscript of Powell's book about his run through the Grand Canyon, they were troubled by the vague sense that something was missing from this great American adventure story. Powell was missing, or at least the passionate Powell that the editors wanted to hear from. The major was a tenacious leader; he meant to survive the canyon and he did survive it, twice. But it wasn't really the adventure he sought, it was the geology. Landforms, not white water, interested Major Powell. Why had the river cut this vast ditch? Or had the river been there before the land rose to form the ditch?

John Wesley Powell's passions were moral. What *was* the right thing to do about the great rivers and the arid lands? The most moving part of Powell's story—Donald Worster tells it admirably—is his struggle, as a poor boy in rural Wisconsin, to get an education, particularly an education in science. Like his idol Lincoln, he would walk miles for a book. He had to teach school in order to get money to go to school, and what training he got, mostly at small Midwestern church schools, was inadequate, particularly in the science where he ended up making his name: geology. Powell was always aware of his limitations as a geologist; part of the thrust of his fund-raising was to get superior geologists such as Dutton and Gilbert on his survey teams.

Powell was wounded at Shiloh; the lower part of his right arm had to be amputated. For the rest of his life he did his best to ignore the fact that he no longer had a right hand. He kept on soldiering, fought at Vicksburg, and, once or twice in the great canyon, even tried one-handed rock climbing. At one point a crew member had to take off his underwear and twist it into a kind of rope in order to rescue Major Powell.

Powell didn't discover the Grand Canyon—Cardenas, one of Coronado's officers, glimpsed it as early as 1540. Escalante and Father Garcés were on the south rim in 1776. Various mountain men had been in the vicinity and Joseph Ives had come up the river partway in 1853. And, of course, there were the Indians, Walipi, Havasupais, Paiutes. Powell, who hadn't supposed anyone could live in the canyon, was startled to discover that the Old Ones, the Anasazi, had been there long before. After his 1869 voyage he became Powell of the Colorado, as surely as Kitchener became Kitchener of Khartoum or Mountbatten Mountbatten of Burma. His celebrity rather annoyed Powell's crewmates, who felt he gave their efforts insufficient acknowledgment. They were right; the major was not much of an acknowledger; but in tracing the Green River down from Wyoming into the Colorado he did eliminate an area of vagueness from the map.

Also, one of the least ambiguous of Powell's achievements was his ethnology. The annual volumes he edited for the US Bureau of Ethnology remain important, and his efforts to secure tribal vocabularies kept hundreds from being lost. Here too he had intelligent assistance.

Powell thought seriously about erosion; he thought seriously about how, or whether, our arid lands could be irrigated. Both Stegner and Worster set up William Gilpin, the boosteristic first territorial governor of Colorado who never met an acre of the West he didn't like, as a straw man and then both shred him; but in fact even in the middle of the nineteenth century there was perplexity about the West. Was it garden or was it desert? The early explorers contradicted one another on this point. The commonsense answer—that some (Lewis and Clark) traveled in wet years and others (Pike and Long) in dry years—was eventually confirmed by tree-ring studies. An army surgeon named George F. Will found a cedar tree near the Little Missouri River that had sprouted around 1339; nearby were some oaks dating from the sixteenth century, and climatological prehistory began to be revealed.

Major Powell didn't have this data, but his experience as a struggling Wisconsin farm boy convinced him that the standard, quarter-section, 160-acre homestead—adequate in well-watered regions—was, in the arid lands, only a slow road to starvation.

Powell had struggled against long odds to become a scientist, and it was in science that he put his faith. He believed that once the problems of aridity were correctly understood, and the possibilities of irrigation correctly estimated, then the people could apply solutions based on scientific fact. If there was only so much water then it was important to decide how best to use it. Powell was a close student of irrigation methods. He admired the water-sharing methods of the New Mexican villages—they have worked for centuries and they still work. He admired the Mormons' cooperative irrigation methods, as well as the successful agricultural practices of the desert Indians, who had less water than anybody but used it brilliantly.

What Powell tried to encourage, through intelligent planning, was what most parents try to teach their children first: sharing. If there was cooperation, if there was sharing, then some of the arid lands could be watered and sustainable settlement made possible. What all the various Greens of our day—the Sierra Club, the Nature Conservancy, Friends of the Earth, Greenpeace, monkey-wrench gangs, etc.—owe to Major Powell is finally an attitude, a conviction that collective stewardship of the earth's resources is possible. To survive we must share, and the sharing needs to be planned.

Though Powell had many bureaucratic rivals, he worked in a time when our bureaucracy was still small. Had he lived into the 1950s and seen what monstrous engines the agencies responsible for sharing these resources had become he might have been shocked. The Bureau of Reclamation was just coming into being when Powell died; by the 1940s its rivalry with the equally aggressive Army Corps of Engineers had changed the face of the American earth to an extent that Major Powell could not have anticipated.

Powell operated in the era of the monopolists, when big speculators, not small bureaucrats, were the enemies of intelligent land classification and water distribution. Powell wanted study to come before settlement, which meant a withholding of public lands, which was anathema—and not merely to the big boys. He thought he could check the monopolists with facts—the major was always a big one for facts. He even tried to reduce the Grand Canyon to a fact—a geologic fact. He underestimated American impatience, and assumed—wrongly—that large interests and small would naturally prefer fact to fable when it came to the arid lands. Surely folks would look at the rainfall statistics and do the right thing. He thought that, in an age of science, people would get enough of romanticizing the West; even in the 1950s Stegner was still harping on the follies of romanticizing such a place:

> It is perhaps unkind to observe that the romanticizing of the West also led to acute political and economic and agricultural blunders, to the sour failure of projects and lives, to the vast avoidable waste of some resources and the monopolization of others, and to a long delay in the reconciling of institutions to realities.

We're nearly fifty years on, and it's not evident to me that institutions and realities are much closer to being reconciled. Certainly they weren't in 1890, when Major Powell's big proposed survey of agricultural and irrigable lands was defeated. The bitter fact the major had to face was that it wasn't just the monopolists who had beaten him, it was in part the dirt farmers too. The American yeomen, the very people who ought to have known better, preferred fable to fact themselves. The major kept his own emotions under such tight rein that he failed to notice that pioneering wasn't rational; it had an emotional component, too. Yes, the arid plains were severe, but so what? The haunting tragic figures of Great Plains literature, Willa Cather's Ántonia, O.E. Rölvaag's Per Hansa, Mari Sandoz's Old Jules, would none of them have listened to Major Powell: they were going anyway, to get their land and test their character against that huge challenge.

It's surprising that John Wesley Powell would have failed to understand this fierce defiance of fact, since he himself, after Shiloh, had fiercely defied it in the matter of his missing right hand. Though a realist on the surface, the major was an idealist underneath. His defeat in 1890 wasn't total—he still had the Geological Survey and the Bureau of Ethnology—but it was bitter nonetheless, because it cut at that idealism which was the wellspring of his life. His neighbor Henry Adams, the Magus of Lafayette Square, would not have been surprised at the major's comeuppance. Here is Henry Adams in *Democracy*, the novel he chose to publish anonymously in 1880:

> ...A delicate mist hangs over Arlington, and softens even the harsh white glare of the Capitol; the struggle of existence seems to abate.... Youthful diplomats, unconscious of their danger, are lured into asking foolish girls to marry them; the blood thaws in the heart and flows out into the veins, like the rills of sparkling water,... as though all the ice and snow on earth,... all the heresy and schism, all the works of the devil, had yielded to the force of love and to the fresh warmth of innocent, lamb-like, confiding virtue. In such a world there should be no guile—but there is a great deal of it notwithstanding.... This is the season when the two whited sepulchres at either end of the Avenue reek with the thick atmosphere of bargain and sale.... Wealth, office, power are at auction. Who bids highest: who hates with most venom? who intrigues with most skill? who has done the dirtiest, the meanest, the darkest, and the most, political work? He shall have his reward.

Chapter 8

PULPMASTER

1.

Now that the gene sleuths have identified the genes for a great many human quirks and compulsions, perhaps it will soon be discovered that there is even a gene for pulp fiction—or, if not a whole gene, at least an errant particle that induces in its victims a kind of lifelong, low-grade logorrhea. The sufferers can't really write well, but they can't stop writing, either. I once saw a letter from an extreme case, Frederick Faust, the so-called "King of the Pulps," who wrote under at least nineteen pseudonyms, the most famous of which is Max Brand. The letter was twenty-eight pages long, single-spaced, and yet Faust had evidently just tossed it off before settling down to work. Frederick Faust's lifetime output has been estimated at thirty million words. But he had aspired to poetry and one of his books of poems was published by Basil Blackwell in Oxford. (Louis L'Amour also aspired to poetry; *his* book of verse was published in Oklahoma City.)

Somewhere, perhaps, reruns of Dr. Kildare—one of Faust's inventions—are still lighting up obscure lives, and a few Max Brand reprints continue to circulate, but the King of the Pulps is long dead and so are his thirty million words. Few pulpers escape immediate oblivion, yet Zane Grey has, and so—perhaps most remarkably—has the German writer Karl May (1842–1912), who set a number of novelettes in the

American West, featuring such Germanic pioneers as Old Shatterhand, Old Surehand, Old Death, Old Wabble, and, of course, Winnetou, the competent Apache sidekick who is probably the source of our own Tonto. Early in life May had been a petty criminal; success, when it came, soon brought out the faker in him. He began to dress like Old Shatterhand, or Kara Ben Nemsi, another of his characters, and to claim that he had actually lived all the events that happen in his books. Peter Gay, in *The Naked Heart*, quotes a letter in which Karl May makes the following claim for his own linguistic skills:

> I speak and write: French, English, Italian, Spanish, Greek, Latin, Hebrew, Romanian, 6 dialects of Arabic, Persian, 2 Kurdish dialects, 6 Chinese dialects, Malaysian, Namqua, a few Sunda idioms, Swahili, Hindustanic, Turkish, and the Indian languages of Sioux, Apaches, Comanches, Snakes, Utahs, Kiowas, in addition to Ketshumanu, 3 south American dialect. Lapp I will not count among them.

Karl May's westerns are some of the dottiest in that vast genre, which is saying a lot, and yet there is a scholarly journal devoted to him (*Jahrbuch der Karl May Gesellschaft*), and an annual festival held in his honor at Bad Segeberg. *Der Spiegel* claimed that he had the greatest influence of any German writer between Goethe and Thomas Mann, and his fans have included Albert Schweitzer, Albert Einstein, Adolf Hitler, and Hermann Hesse. Schweitzer, Einstein, and Hitler very likely were subject to bouts of brain fatigue severe enough that Karl May's weird, quasi-Wagnerian fictions about the American West might have made a likely antidote—but Hermann Hesse? And yet it was Hesse who said that May's work represents "a type of literature that is indispensable and eternal." Besides that, for what it's worth, the German director Carl Zuckmayer, co-screenwriter on *The Blue Angel*, named his daughter Winnetou.

The overwhelming popularity of utterly ridiculous pulp fiction is a matter to give one pause, and pause over it we will, a little later. For now it is a relief to leave the sons of Wotan and examine the homelier contours of our own Zane Grey, born Gray—once grown both he and his brother opted for that stylish English "e"—who was first a dentist and a baseball player, then a writer, and finally a sports fisherman of considerable renown.

Stephen May—no kin, I guess, to Karl—has now written two readable books about Zane Grey. The first, *Zane Grey: Romancing the West*, is a study of the fiction in relation to its (mainly) western background; the second, *Maverick Heart*, is a biography.[1] Professor May has not escaped entirely unscathed from a too-close association with Zane Grey's cliché-heavy style, the result being comments such as "Blazing like a meteor, he soared through life," but he is usually more sensible than that, and is even fair enough to quote Heywood Broun's to my mind accurate remark that "the substance of any two Zane Grey books could be written upon the back of a postage stamp."

Professor May is annoyed by the scorn that has been heaped on Zane Grey's writing, and yet, by quoting liberally from the books themselves, unfortunately ensures that more scorn will be heaped. He is careless enough, for example, to offer this compliment early in *Maverick Heart*:

> In my mind, most of Grey's work discussed in this book contains splendid description, insightful narration, frequent humor, surprising vitality, pungent wit, and provocative philosophy.

It might be best to start with the provocative philosophy and work back toward the splendid description:

---

1. *Zane Grey: Romancing the West* (Ohio University Press, 1997); *Maverick Heart: The Further Adventures of Zane Grey* (Ohio University Press, 2000).

> A man can die. He is glorious when he calmly accepts death; but when he fights like a tiger, when he stands at bay his back to the wall, a broken weapon in his hand, bloody, defiant, game to the end, then he is sublime.... Then he is avenged even in his death.

Or:

> She was woman with all a woman's charm to bewitch, to twine round the strength of men as the ivy encircles the oak... with all a woman's wilful burning love....
>
> At last so much of life was intelligible to him. The renegade committed his worst crimes because even in his outlawed, homeless state, he couldn't exist without the companionship, if not the love, of a woman.

Examples of pungent wit, surprising vitality, and frequent humor I cannot immediately locate, but we might try this for insightful narration:

> "*Don't anybody move!*"
>
> Like a steel whip this voice cut the silence. It belonged to Blue. Jean swiftly bent to put his eye to a crack in the door. Most of those visible seemed to have been frozen into unnatural positions. Jorth stood rather in front of his men, hatless and coatless, his arm outstretched, and his dark profile set toward a little man just inside the door. This man was Blue. Jean needed only one flashing look at Blue's face, at his leveled, quivering guns, to understand why he had chosen this trick.
>
> "Who're—you?" demanded Jorth, in husky pants.

And here's the splendid description:

> Late in the afternoon I slipped off down the canyon, taking Haught's rifle for safety rather than a desire to kill anything. By no means was it impossible to meet a bad bear in the forest.... Like coming home again was it to enter that forest.... What cool, sweet, fresh smell this woody, leafy, earthy, dry, grassy, odorous fragrance, dominated by the scent of pine.... This golden-green forest, barred by sunlight, canopied by the blue sky, and melodious with its soughing moan of wind, absolutely filled me with content and happiness.

I didn't find these four passages in Zane Grey's books—I found them in Professor May's two studies, quoted, it would seem, with approval. As prose, though, I think they are entirely consistent with thousands of pages of Zane Grey's writing, spread through more than eighty books. Why Stephen May thinks it's good writing is hard to know, since almost any passage in any of Zane Grey's books makes it cruelly obvious that the man failed to master even the most basic unit of his craft: the prose sentence.

Once he became successful, with the publication of *The Heritage of the Desert* in 1910, Zane Grey left the pulps behind him and wrote mainly for the vastly more lucrative slicks. His regular customers were *Country Gentleman*, *McClures*, *Cosmopolitan*, *Collier's*, *Coronet*, *The Ladies Home Journal*, etc.; the respectable house of Harper published his books. But, wherever he published, Zane Grey still wrote like a pulper, at top speed, like Frederick Faust. It's not evident from the prose that Zane Grey even noticed sentences—he was scribbling them off too fast—and, after 1905, it didn't matter so much, because in that year he married Dolly Roth, a woman as patient as he was impatient, and not merely in the matter of prose, either. Dolly, who once described herself to her (absent) husband as "the 'alonest' person I've ever met, no matter how many people are around me," cleaned up Grey's hasty manuscripts, punctuated them, edited them, and sold them. She was wife, editor, and agent all in one. Once, in his usual rush, Grey sent off a story without letting Dolly work on it; to his chagrin it was immediately rejected. Dolly worked on it and sold it. She got to know the various magazine editors well, and kept a close eye on the market. In the boom days of the Twenties she once got her husband as much as $80,000 for a serialization. And where was Zane while Dolly was so ably managing his literary affairs? Zane was usually gone fishing.

2.

Was Zane Grey primarily a writer who fished, or was he, essentially, a fisherman who wrote? In his youth he was a pretty good baseball player, playing for summer leagues in Ohio, Michigan, and New Jersey; he loved baseball and wrote three baseball books for boys, but, from boyhood in the 1870s until his death in 1939, the activity Zane Grey loved best was fishing. Literary fame and the fortune that came with it enabled him to fish for larger and larger fish in more and more distant waters. He fished off Nova Scotia, Mexico, Tahiti, Bora Bora, Tonga, Australia, and New Zealand; in 1936 he landed a tiger shark off Sydney that weighed 1,036 pounds. Between 1924 and 1936 he held fourteen deep-sea fishing records. After he became interested in sharks he even starred in a movie called *White Death*, a killer-shark movie that anticipated *Jaws* by some forty years. Grey himself took what became the Robert Shaw role, the shark hunter brought in to save the village.

White Death flopped, much to Grey's annoyance, but he had very little to complain about where movies were concerned, being far and away the most-filmed American author. To date one hundred and eleven movies have been made from his books, which means that many of them have been filmed twice, as silents and again as talkies.

Riders of the Purple Sage was remade as recently as 1996 and did respectable business, too.

Zane Grey's many fishing trips kept him away from home for as much as six or eight months at a time, one reason Dolly Grey felt herself to be the "alonest" person she had ever met. Grey usually had female company on his trips, young female company for the most part, a situation Dolly only just managed to tolerate. When she did explode it was usually because one of these "secretaries" had attempted to usurp her work as an editor of her husband's writing, a task she was still pressing on with as late as 1953, fourteen years after his death.

Ernest Hemingway was a literary man who liked to hunt and fish. The hunting and fishing were important to him, but not as important as the writing—not even close. Zane Grey was the other way around. He wrote as rapidly as possible, trusting to his wife to tidy up his manuscripts, and then he got back to his fishing. He wrote and published more than eighty books without ever quite becoming a literary man. Even Professor May has an uneasy sense of this, admitting, finally, that Zane Grey never matured as a novelist; he thinks Grey will probably be remembered as a folklorist, but this I doubt. Zane Grey was a very crude fabulist, not a folklorist; he was an enormously popular pulp writer who came along at a time when "outdoor" writing was in demand, thus enabling him to sell his work to the slicks, make a lot of money, and catch some very large fish.

I'm aware, though, that a listing of Zane Grey's deficiencies as a writer doesn't settle all the questions. Virtually all his books are still in print, even the boys' books and even his awkward first novel, *Betty Zane*, first published in 1903. What if Hermann Hesse is right to remark that such literature as Zane Grey and Karl May produced is indispensable? What, exactly, is the element of indispensability in these apparently childish creations?

There is a passage in *Beginning Again*, the third volume of Leonard Woolf's autobiography, that might contain a clue. He is writing about Mrs. Funnell, a country woman who worked for the Woolfs in Sussex:

> Mrs. Funnell was a woman of iron will, but, in so far as her hard life allowed it, of good will. She became quite fond of Virginia, and, to a much lesser degree, of me. She brought up a family, in spotless cleanliness and considerable fear of their mother, on the starvation wages of her husband. Within the limits of her profound ignorance of the world outside of a four-mile radius of her cottage... she had sagacity, understanding, curiosity, intelligence. I think she had scarcely ever read a book, but one day one of our visitors left a copy of Ethel M. Dell's *The Way of an Eagle* in our kitchen and Mrs. Funnell became completely engrossed in it—it was my first experience of the mysterious, devastating power of the great born best seller, which acts like a force of nature... upon the mind and heart of unsophisticated millions.
>
> I only once saw Mrs. Funnell in any way upset.... One evening there was a knock on the sitting room door and there stood Mrs. Funnell again, obviously "in a state," a dark, fierce, but worried look on her broad, lined, handsome face. Without beating around the bush she told us that her unmarried daughter was at that moment giving birth to a child.... So bare was the home of a Sussex shepherd 50 years ago that she had not the necessary towels, basins, cans, and she had come to borrow them from us. The child was safely delivered, the father being, it was said, the bailiff, but Mrs. Funnell never mentioned the subject again.

Chapter 9

JANET LEWIS

1.

In 1922 the printer-typographer Monroe Wheeler, who would go on to have a long and distinguished career with MoMA, set off to be a young-man-about-Europe. He was determined to publish poetry and publish it elegantly, to which end he established (first in Germany) an imprint called Manikin, under which he issued three booklets of verse. The first, *The Indians in the Woods*, was by a young Midwestern poet named Janet Lewis; William Carlos Williams's *Go Go* was the second; the third and last was *Marriage*, by Marianne Moore.

Not long before he left Illinois, Wheeler had got his feet wet typographically, so to speak, by publishing two books of verse now not easily secured: *The Bitterns*, by his friend Glenway Westcott, and *The Immobile Wind*, by a young teacher of languages named Arthur Yvor Winters, who had, not long before, been released from the Sunmount Sanatorium in Santa Fe, where he recovered from a serious bout with tuberculosis. Young Winters was soon to go off to Moscow, Idaho, to take the only teaching job he could get, but, on a trip to Chicago, he met Janet Lewis. Monroe Wheeler was one link, poetry a second, and tuberculosis a third, for Janet Lewis too was soon forced to go off to Sunmount, where—after nearly five years—she also recovered. Hers was a close call. The two married in 1926—Janet Lewis was still in Sunmount and Yvor Winters still teaching in Idaho, from whence he carried on an intense correspondence, largely about poetics, with Hart Crane, Allen Tate, and others. Once Janet Lewis was well, the young couple moved to California and Winters took up the professorship at Stanford that he was to hold for the rest of his life.

Together the two writers raised children (two), Airedales and goats (many), and—one might say—poets: ranks upon ranks of poets who came to learn from Winters; in their memoirs he is still legend. He wrote his books, Janet wrote hers. To his enemies in criticism—at various times they included the Agrarians (particularly John Crowe Ransom), Eliot, Pound, R. P. Blackmur, and many others—Yvor Winters was a bruiser, a kind of absolutist gladiator who struck often and with considerable accuracy at flaws in a poem or a critical system. To poets—from Hart Crane on to J. V. Cunningham, Donald Justice, Donald Hall, Thom Gunn, Ann Stanford, Robert Haas, and many others—he was a kind of Apostle, though of course they felt varying degrees of allegiance to his beliefs about poetry and of attachment to the man himself; but to Janet Lewis he was, for forty-two years, a much-treasured husband, as she makes clear in an audiotape made twenty years after his death. The cut of that grief went very deep; his name, A. Yvor Winters, is still on the mailbox of their modest house in Los Altos.

Of all the above mentioned, Wheeler and Westcott, Crane, Tate, Williams, Marianne Moore, and Yvor Winters are gone, but Janet Lewis lives on, for the most part happily, in Los Altos; her sight has weakened but not her spirit. She has published poetry in every decade of this century except the first, poetry that has never lacked for champions. One of the most ardent, at present, is Thom

Gunn, who had this to say about her most recent collection, *Dear Past*:[1]

> I think she should be getting the closest attention. In this collection of old age, almost incredibly, she is simultaneously as stringent and sweet-natured, as sharp and generous as she was throughout the *Collected Poems*. She is as ever deceptively simple. That is, hers is the best kind of simplicity, because it contains an implied complexity....

Dear Past reprints poems published between 1918 and 1991, a wingspan all but incredible, and made the more so by the clarity and authority of a voice she has sustained for so long: a voice that is considered, lucid, spare, and tough on itself in a high midwestern way. Though perhaps less imperatively than her husband, she too has touched many poets, from the time of Hart Crane to the time of Robert Haas. Of her verse she has kept and reprinted only about a poem a year, taking her time and finishing her work; luckily she has been granted a great deal of time to take.

In addition to the poetry Janet Lewis has written two children's books, six books of prose, four libretti, and a number of chorales. Though I am mainly concerned in this essay to applaud and perhaps bring new readers to the three remarkable historical novels she published between 1941 and 1959, I do think that Janet Lewis's more than eighty years of vigorous, variegated, and steady devotion to literature deserves a salute. She is a striking example of a quiet talent working quietly through almost the entirety of a noisy, celebrity-heavy century.

---

1. *Dear Past and Other Poems, 1919–1994* (Robert L. Barth, 1995).

From so much attention one would expect a masterpiece, and it too is there, *The Wife of Martin Guerre* (1941),[2] the story of an artifice so skillful, so confusing to its victims, that simple honesty is defeated and a good woman brought to ruin.[3] It's a short novel that can run with *Billy Budd*, *The Spoils of Poynton*, *Seize the Day*, or any other of the thoroughbred novellas that might be brought to the gate.

In a statement given to Stanley Kunitz and Howard Haycraft for the 1955 edition of that still-invaluable reference work *Twentieth Century Authors*, Janet Lewis made a couple of intriguing statements. She mentions her husband's standing as a breeder of Airedales, but says nothing about his fame as a literary critic, encouraging us to suspect that the much-feared Yvor Winters, one of the hardest hitters of the bare-knucklers who slugged it out in the bloody pit of criticism as it was in the Thirties and Forties, may really have put more of his heart into his dogs. About herself she has this to say:

> I have lived a life rather lacking in "events" but with a rich and in the main very happy background. This sort of life does not provide a very interesting brief biography. The interest is chiefly in the background, which can't be treated briefly and still be interesting.

Though that statement was made forty-three years ago, I doubt she would modify it much today.

---

2. Ohio University Press/Swallow Press, 1984.

3. For a skillful unraveling of the complex history behind the Martin Guerre story, readers are referred to *The Return of Martin Guerre*, by Natalie Zemon Davis (Harvard University Press, 1983).

2.

That life began in Chicago, in 1899. (Janet, who is often amused, was particularly amused recently when a schoolgirl pointed out that if she makes it another couple of years she'll have lived in three centuries.) Her father, Edwin Herbert Lewis, a teacher and writer, encouraged his children's artistic leanings from the first. Her brother, Herbert Lewis, designed the dust jacket and endpapers for her first work of prose, *The Invasion* (1931).[4] She went to the same Oak Park high school as Hemingway, at the same time, and was friends with his sister Marcelline, who was in her French club. "So I heard a lot about Ernie," she says now. She and Hemingway each have a poem in the January 1923 issue of *Poetry*.

The Lewises, like the Hemingways, had a summer place up in Michigan, in the Lewises' case way up, on an island in the St. Mary's River, midway between Mackinac and the Sault Ste. Marie. She includes three or four up-in-Michigan stories in the collection *Goodbye, Son*,[5] stories which contrast interestingly with Hemingway's Michigan stories. The emotional sawteeth beneath the clear surface of Hemingway's prose are not there in Janet Lewis, though, like as not, her stories are more overtly tragic than his. In stories such as "Proserpina," "River," and "Nell," the local tragedies and misfortunes—a kindly drunk's drowning, an appealing young woman self-thwarted—are ringed with a soft midwestern melancholy closer in tone to Sherwood Anderson or Edgar Lee Masters than to the pre-existential edginess of Hemingway. The St. Mary's River country she describes in *The Invasion* is that country unspoiled, as it was in the eighteenth and nineteenth centuries; but in his "Big Two-

4. Michigan State University Press, 1998.

5. Ohio University Press/Swallow Press, 1986.

Hearted River" the same country is despoiled, the scarred terrain a natural metaphor for burnout. Janet Lewis had been happy in Michigan; she saw it as a fullness, whereas for Hemingway it seemed to accentuate the absences in life.

Another difference is that her interest in Michigan, once it went beyond the responses of an enraptured child on a summer outing, was historical. She made Ojibway friends, and was soon deep in the history of that much-disputed region: first Indian, then French, then British, then American, and always, after the French arrived, *metis*. *The Invasion* is an imaginative history of the founding Johnston family, a family in which Scotch-Irish and Indian blood soon mixed. It happened to be the family, too, into which the pioneering ethnographer Henry Schoolcraft married, a distant result of which was *Hiawatha*, Mr. Longfellow having depended more than a little on Henry Schoolcraft's researches. Janet Lewis has always insisted that *The Invasion* is a "narrative," not a novel; whatever one calls it, it is a confident, pungently written first book, with close attention paid to the densities, the shading, and the smells of the northern forests and its peoples, at the time when the Americans first came to them.

That Janet Lewis, the woman, was less depressed than her schoolmate Ernest Hemingway is not to suggest that her work is Pollyanna-ish; the message of her major fiction is very dark indeed. She comes back again and again to the fate of honesty in a violent world. Her novels are tragedies, and this despite the fact that she was the product of a happy family, and, as a wife and mother, helped mold a happy family. The calm of her prose, and of the best of her verse, is a hard-won—indeed, a philosophic—calm. No one, saint or poet, could have lived through almost the entire twentieth century—or any century—and remained undisturbed. It is what she makes of her disturbances, as she struggles to keep her balance and do her duty, that is impressive. Not for nothing was the little magazine that she and her husband published for a single year in the late Twenties called

The Gyroscope: the instrument that spins and yet does not lose its balance.

Hart Crane was awed by Yvor Winters's learning—why, he could even read Portuguese!—and so impressed by his sensitivity to poetry that he allowed him to midwife *The Bridge*, rather as Pound had midwifed *The Waste Land*; and, though there was an ugly quarrel once Winters's harsh, disappointed review of the finished poem came out, Crane had not been entirely wrong to trust Winters's ear and his sensitivity. Yvor Winters from the first put the act of evaluation at the center of his critical practice. In *The Armed Vision* Stanley Edgar Hyman poked fun at some of Winters's wilder overestimations—Elizabeth Baryush, Jones Very, Sturge Moore—but he still respected Winters's force as a critic. This essay is about Janet Lewis, not Yvor Winters, but it is, I think, of interest that all Janet Lewis's major fiction hinges on the difficulty of just and accurate evaluation, not merely in the law but in the mundane circumstances of everyday life, where the consequences of misevaluation are apt to be more destructive than they usually are in literary criticism. Something of the evaluative habits of the poet-critic husband soaked deep into the creative practices of the poet-novelist wife.

The Winterses were not wealthy; professors were not then superstars. Janet Lewis wanted to write fiction for magazines that paid money, so as to add her tiny bit to the family coffers. But she was not by nature a good plotter, and was only now and then able to sell something to the slicks. Sometime in the Thirties Yvor Winters was lent an old law book, a nineteenth-century compilation of famous cases of circumstantial evidence. At some point Winters handed the book to his wife, thinking there might be something in it that would help her with her plots.

Did it ever! Though not quickly. At first she merely took notes and reflected, but the notes sprouted and in time she produced the three novels of her maturity: *The Wife of Martin Guerre* (1941), *The Trial of Sören Qvist* (1947),[6] and *The Ghost of Monsieur Scarron* (1959).[7] Though it is not likely that the family finances were much affected, Janet Lewis *did* learn to plot. She tells three stories in which the fate of honest people depends on their ability or inability to correctly evaluate the confusing body of evidence that life presents us as we go rushing through it. In all three cases it is the human, not the judicial, misevaluation that makes the books so powerful.

3.

Whoa, though. Despite the steady and loyal readership these three novels have won her, Janet Lewis thinks of herself mostly as a poet. Poetry is what she began with and what she still has now. She started with Imagism, the vogue of her youth, but she soon developed a less impersonal, more individual, and more complex poetic style. One would be foolish to try to guess where she'll finish up, since so far she's shown no inclination to finish at all. She has always looked closely, and with delight, at the natural world and has rendered it vividly both in verse and prose. Some of her poems have come from contemplation of her garden, or her goats, or just the morning light:

> *The path*
> *The Spider makes through the air,*
> *Invisible,*
> *Until the light touches it.*
> *The path*
> *The light takes through the air, invisible,*
> *Until it finds the spider's web.*

---

6. Ohio University Press/Swallow Press, 2000.

7. Ohio University Press/Swallow Press, 1981.

I won't attempt to follow Janet Lewis through the many decades of adding and subtracting, winnowing and honing, that have boiled down to the poems in her most recent selection, but I would like to link in a brief way one set or sequence of poems to the prime concerns of her fiction, specifically her powerful desire for balance; she doesn't want to be swept away, or altered in her nature, however violent or whatever the character of the storms that strike her. This need for balance doesn't deny sentiment—she has plenty of that—but attempts to secure for sentiment its due dignity.[8]

In the interview mentioned earlier, she makes clear that the death of Yvor Winters was a devastating blow; for a time after it she wrote nothing. But she did go back to the desert, to the places of the pueblo peoples, the Hopi and Navajo, peoples who appear to live in harmony with the eternal simplicities: sun, stone, sky. She ponders a fossil:

> *In quiet dark transformed to stone,*
> *Cell after cell to crystal grown,*
> *The pattern stays, the substance gone. . . .*

And, in a museum in Tucson, contemplates—at first with envy—the mummy of a small Anasazi woman:

> *How, unconfused, she met the morning sun,*
> *And the pure sky of night,*
> *Knowing no land beyond the great horizons . . .*

But later she learns of the massacre at Awatobi (1700), where defenders of the old gods wiped out a village that had accepted the new gods

8. *Landscape, Memory, and the Poetry of Janet Lewis*, by Brigitte Carnochan, an excellent short study, was published by the Stanford Libraries and English Department in 1995.

of the Spaniards; she realizes that the little woman may not have been spared confusion and terror after all:

Men of Awátobi,
Killed by men of the Three Mesas,
By arrow, by fire,
Betrayed, trapped in their own kivas.

. . .

The men of the Three Mesas,
In terror for the peace of the great kachinas
Who hold the world together,
Who hold creation in balance,
Took council, acted. . . .

In bereavement Janet Lewis sought, even as she had in the happy *Gyroscope* years, the secret of things that move but are not changed:

The sunlight pours unshaken through the wind . . .

And she takes a poet's delight in the fact that the Navajo, who simplify many things, cannot reduce water to one name:

Tsaile, Chinle,
Water flowing in, flowing out.

Slow water caught in a pool,
Caught in a gourd;
Water upon the lips, in the throat,
Falling upon long hair
Loosened in ceremony;
Fringes of rain sweeping darkly
From the dark side of a cloud,

Riding the air in sunlight,
Issuing cold from a rock,
Transparent as air, or darkened
With earth, bloodstained, grief-heavy;

In a country of no dew, snow
Softly piled, or stinging
in bitter wind...

The earth and the sky were constant,
But water,
How could they name it with one name?

In poetry Janet Lewis developed a singularity of voice over time, but in prose she was from the first strikingly confident. Here is the opening paragraph of *The Invasion*; we are on the plains of Abraham in 1759:

> That September day the English appeared so suddenly that they seemed to have dropped from the sky; appeared, and fired. A warm rain fell now and again upon the troops, and the smoke from the rifles lay in long white streamers, dissipating slowly. The noise of the rifles, reflected from the running water and from the cliffs, was something like thunder, but the rain was too quiet. And running, for the French, had become almost more important than fighting. The head of Montcalm lay upon the breast of Ma-mongazid, the young Ojibway, the dark sorrowful face, with its war paint of vermilion and white, intent above the French face graying rapidly. Presently they took the Marquis to the hospital in St. Charles, where he died. Ma-mongazid with his warriors in thirty bark canoes returned to pointe Chegoimegon through the yellowing woods and increasing storms of autumn. The rule of the French was over, the province of Michilimackinac had become the

> Northwest Territory. The Ojibways called the English Saugaunosh, the Dropped-From-The-Clouds, and regretted the French.

With similar confidence she brings us to Jutland in the early seventeenth century, as she opens the story of the parson of Vejlby, Sören Qvist:

> The inn lay in a hollow, the low hill, wooded with leafless beech trees, rising behind it in a gentle round just high enough to break the good draft from the inn chimneys, so that on this chill day the smoke rose a little and then fell downward. The air was clouded with dampness. It was late November, late in the afternoon, but no sunlight came from the west, and to the east the sky was walled with cloud where the cold fog thickened above the shores of Jutland. There was the smell of sea in the air even these few miles inland, but the foot traveler who had come upon sight of the inn had been so close to the sea for so many days now that he was unaware of the salty fragrance....

and to Gascony almost a century earlier, as she begins *Martin Guerre*:

> One morning in January of 1539, a wedding was celebrated in the village of Artigues. That night the two children who had been espoused to one another lay in bed in the house of the groom's father. They were Bertrande de Rols, aged eleven years, and Martin Guerre, who was no older, both offspring of rich peasant families as ancient, as feudal and as proud as any of the great seignorial houses of Gascony. The room was cold. Outside the snow lay thinly over the stony ground, or, gathered into long shallow drifts at the corners of the houses, left the earth bare. But higher it extended upward in great sheets and dunes,

> mantling the ridges and choking the wooded valleys, toward the peak of La Bacanère and the long ridge of Le Burat, and to the south, beyond the long valley of Luchon, the granite Maladetta stood sheathed in ice and snow. . . .

The movement backward, into earlier centuries, which might inhibit many writers, seems to excite Janet Lewis and also to increase her assurance. When she comes into her own time, as she does in her one conventional novel of manners, *Against a Darkening Sky* (1943), set in Santa Clara County during the Depression, she is noticeably less confident. The heroine of that book is introduced to us as Mary Perrault, but is often thereafter called Mrs. Perrault, as if the author is not sure just how much intimacy she should assume with her main character.

In a way the three historical novels, all based on actual cases in the law, are legal briefs brought to life, the novelist being a prosecutor whose sympathies are nonetheless with the accused; and the accused, in all cases, become the condemned. There is nothing quite like these three books in our fiction; such echoes as there are are French, particularly Stendhal. All the central characters, whether Bertrande de Rols, or Pastor Sören, or the honest bookbinder Jean Larcher, are threatened by judicial confusion over circumstantial evidence, but the brilliance of the pattern is the way in which Janet Lewis shows that none of the three would ever have been in court in the first place had they themselves not made similar misjudgments when confronted with the rushing mass of circumstantial evidence in everyday life.

Perhaps the best example of such normal error occurs in *The Ghost of Monsieur Scarron*. Paul Damas, the apprentice bookbinder who has seduced his master's wife, Marianne, loses a button from his shirt:

> One day in midsummer, Paul and Marianne being alone in the bindery, Paul remarked that he had lost a button from his shirt, and Marianne offered to sew it on for him.

It seemed an innocent activity, especially in view of their relationship. She performed the task deftly and quickly, then looked about for her scissors to snip the thread. Not finding them, "Lend me your knife," she said to Paul. "No, never mind," and, bending toward him, she bit the thread. The action brought her head against his breast. Perhaps she held it there the fraction of a moment longer than was necessary. It seemed to Paul that she delayed the moment, for, looking over her head, he met the surprised gaze of his master. Jean had returned, with no undue quietness of step, with no intention of taking anyone unawares, but absorbed in themselves, neither Paul nor Marianne had heard the opening of the door or the advancing step. A rigidity in Paul warned Marianne of something amiss. She lifted her head, looked first at Paul, then followed his glance toward her husband.

Midday, midsummer, the air was warm and moist after a morning shower. Marianne had discarded her cap and fichu. Her arms were bare almost to the shoulder, as she had pushed back her sleeves. The air, the informality of the moment, the two figures standing like one in a rectangle of sunlight, all combined to give Jean an impression of what was in fact the truth. But the moment itself was innocent.

A sense of revelation rushed upon him, bringing to mind a hundred hitherto unquestioned gestures, poses, inflections. They were lovers, these two. He had taken his wife in adultery.... He stopped dead where he stood. Then the moment resolved itself naturally, without drama. Marianne came toward him, holding on the middle finger of the hand poised above her, her silver thimble....

"I mislaid my scissors," she said. "I had to use my teeth."

...Jean's fear and knowledge turned about him and then leveled into an illusion. Nothing was wrong....

There you have the pregnant, and, in this case, fatal, error. Jean Larcher had read the action correctly, had seen the avidity in his wife's face and in her bite; and yet he talks himself out of it. Had he held to his true perception and thrown his adulterous wife and treacherous apprentice out at this juncture, he would have saved himself torture and death. But he suborned his own sound judgment, in this case tragically.

The human tendency to dissuade oneself from accurate insight surfaces rather more complexly in the story of Sören Qvist, a good pastor at war with himself because of his uncontrollable angers. Pastor Sören has a real enemy, one Morten Bruus, who tricks him, but it is really the force of the Pastor's faith-driven self-accusation that causes the trick to work: he convinces himself that he has killed Morten Bruus's brother, though the brother, in fact, is not dead.

Reading the three novels in a line, from *The Wife of Martin Guerre* to *The Ghost of Monsieur Scarron*, is a powerful experience. Though all three were based on actual cases in the law, their power is literary not legal. In each story a son leaves home because of strife with the father, and returns too late to save the family. In each the ruin of an honest person is complete, and in each there is a fully and vividly realized woman who finds herself twisting helplessly in the dilemmas posed by love and duty. To each of these women—Bertrande de Rols, Anna Sörensdaughter, and Marianne Larcher—Janet Lewis might say what she says to the mummy of the Anasazi woman in Tucson, "my sister, my friend," for she knows these women: their feelings, their gestures, their happiness, their changeability, and their stunned helplessness as they see doom approaching.

Anna Sörensdaughter has her happiness destroyed when the young judge she loves and is engaged to marry has to pass the sentence of death on her father. Bertrande de Rols must finally accuse the nice imposter who is kind to her because she can but for so long live a lie; she chooses truth over love and then is dismissed with perfect coldness when the real Martin Guerre comes back and discovers that she has dishonored him. Marianne Larcher is the weakest of the three women, so physically in thrall to the young apprentice that she will do anything for him; but she is no less appealing for being blindly dependent, even though it results in her good husband being condemned. The last words of the Martin Guerre story might serve as ending for all these novels:

> Of Martin Guerre no more is recorded, whether he returned to the wars or remained in Artigues, nor is there further record of Bertrande de Rols, his wife. But when love and hate have together exhausted the soul, the body seldom endures for long.

In the old law book her husband lent her, Janet Lewis discerned a great theme: the limitations of human judgment, not merely between judge and accused but between husband and wife, father and son, king and counselor (for it was a little burlesque in the manner of the late Monsieur Scarron, insulting Madame de Maintenon, that resulted in the execution of the honest bookbinder). She discerned it and, for a span of some twenty years in her long life, had the intelligence, the persistence, and the force to be equal to it.

Auden reminded us definitively that it's language Time worships: not wisdom or innocence or physical beauty or, I would add, length of life. Janet Lewis has indeed lived a long time, but what is important is that all through that long time she has continued to tell the stories that have meant something to her in a manner all her own, and with a distinction of language that will carry them forward to startle and delight readers yet to come.

4.

Though I was at Stanford in 1960 I failed to meet Janet Lewis. Now and then I would see her husband proceeding in Johnsonian fashion through the college, often with a Boswell or two tugging at his sleeves, but, at the time, it was *her* work that excited me, an excitement that came back with its old force when I reread her recently.

So I ventured a letter and, to my delight, she promptly called me in Texas and invited me to dinner on Valentine's Day of 1998. She didn't sound like the grandmother of fiction, either, when she called; she just sounded like a well-spoken woman who was curious about what a writer from Texas would make of her work.

I arrived at her home in Los Altos hand in hand with El Niño; the abundant vegetation that must once have enticed her goats dripped from every leaf and stem. I felt like the person who was going to meet the person who had once seen Shelley plain—Shelley in this case being Hart Crane, who had visited the Winterses at Christmas in 1927. Janet, still convalescent, gave him tea in her bedroom, which, at the time, she was rarely allowed to leave. "Oh yes," she said, when I mentioned that tea. "He was very polite." Despite the breach that occurred over her husband's review of *The Bridge*, the Winterses were both deeply grieved when Hart Crane killed himself by jumping off the boat.

Janet too is very polite, but she's neither fussy nor chilly. She's lived in that smallish but cheerful house for sixty-four years and is thoroughly the mistress of it; there she raised her family, there she watched war come and war be over, there she entertained generations of poets, artists, musicians, and even the occasional lepidopterist such as Vladimir Nabokov, who showed up at her door with his butterfly net one day in 1941. The Nabokovs and the Winterses hit it off; the exiles came often for meals. I had heard that Nabokov enjoyed himself so much in her kitchen that he sometimes helped her wash up;

when I asked her about this she chuckled and said, "Why, I wouldn't be surprised if he had."

I had hardly said hello when we were off through the streaming backyard to the small, detached study where she and Yvor Winters did their writing; an old Royal typewriter sits as a reminder of those days. On the walls, casually tacked up, were photographs of a number of noble Airedales and several slightly less noble poets, one or two of them so obscure that neither of us could quite puzzle out who they might be. A sketch of Pound was by one window; a lovely photograph of Janet as a young woman hung from a nail. Janet remarked that the goats came into her life at a time when she was too weak to write but liked to sketch; Yvor Winters went down the road and bought a couple of goats, so his wife could have something to sketch besides Airedales.

Later, two gifted men friends turned up and cooked a delicious meal, which we ate at the small table in her kitchen. Once, on the audiotape, when a young interviewer was asking her how she got the details right in her historical fiction, Janet talked for a bit about looking at Breughel and reading lots of histories, but then she dropped from the highfalutin' and merely said, "I've always liked kitchens"; it is as if she is saying that from her own bright kitchen, where Vladimir Nabokov once wielded a dish towel, she can imagine all kitchens, as her fiction—filled with kitchens—demonstrates.

In the company of most people who are brushing a century, ignoring their age requires conscious effort; but when Janet Lewis is discussing a book or remembering a visit or a trip, or describing northern Michigan as it was in her girlhood, *remembering* that she's elderly is what takes the conscious effort. Perhaps the fact that her sickness was so nearly mortal, that she lived for five years of her young womanhood with death as a near-neighbor, has left her unimpressed that it's in the neighborhood still. Though she is reasonably cautious, and is attended by squadrons of friends, who do their attending for the rich reward of her company, there is also a slightly mischievous, slightly devil-may-care, I'll-go-when-I'm-good-and-ready air about her. It's as if that terribly early struggle has bought her a little exemption, and she knows it, and she means to enjoy her privileges to the full.

The four of us finished the meal very companionably, had dessert, had more tea. Janet probed around in a bookcase and found an essay on her poetry that she thought I might like to read. I took it and wandered back to my motel on the Camino, thrilled. A great lady of American letters had—for the space of an evening—been my valentine.

Chapter 10

THE AMERICAN EPIC

The journey of the Corps of Discovery, under the command of Captains Meriwether Lewis and William Clark, across the American West to the Pacific Ocean and back in the years 1804–1806 seems to me to have been our first really American adventure, one that also produced our only really American epic, *The Journals of the Lewis and Clark Expedition*,[1] now at last available in a superbly edited, easily read edition in twelve volumes (of an eventual thirteen), almost two centuries after the Corps of Discovery set out.

Of course the West was aboil with explorers from the 1520s on: Cabeza de Vaca, Coronado, De Soto, and other Spaniards from the south and southwest; a host of French coming down through the Great Lakes to the Mississippi, Father Marquette, LaSalle, with the La Vérendrye family a little farther west in 1738–1741. Escalante was at the Grand Canyon while the Revolutionary War was being fought. Santa Fe already gleamed as the New World Samarkand, though there was as yet no consensus among the caravaners as to how to get there. Pedro Vial startled his Spanish superiors in 1792 by informing them that it was only twenty-five days across from Santa

1. Edited by Gary E. Moulton (University of Nebraska Press, 1983–1999).

Fe to the Missouri River—or at least it was if one could avoid being captured by Indians, as he had been. His superiors had rather hoped that the Americans were farther away.

The remarkable, too-little-known Canadian explorer David Thompson was already quietly probing the Columbia River system, and even slipped down to the Mandan villages in 1797, where French traders had long been active. The Mandan villages were near present-day Bismarck, North Dakota; Lewis and Clark wintered there in 1804–1805, with representatives of both the Hudson's Bay Company and the Northwest Company right there with them. The polite French trader François-Antoine Larocque did his best to be civil to the Americans, but Larocque worked for the British and Captain Lewis was a confirmed Anglophobe. There was tension, but the trading went on in such a lively fashion that an astute visionary might have even foreseen the outlet malls that dot that same area today.

But these men—De Vaca, Coronado, De Soto, La Salle, the Vérendryes, Vial, David Thompson, Larocque, and many, many more—were all Europeans, or else were representing European countries or companies. Lewis and Clark were our own boys, working for Mr. Jefferson and the greater glory of the young republic. Monsieur Larocque, for all his civility, was probably a little startled to see Americans at the Mandan villages so soon, just as Pedro Vial's bosses had been shocked to hear that the Americans were only a month from their doorstep. For Spain's and France's and England's western interests, the arrival of Lewis and Clark at the big trade depot of the Mandans was the beginning of the end. More remarkably, they would have been there even *without* the Louisiana Purchase—Captain Lewis was already on his way to Pittsburgh to pick up his boat when *that* plum dropped in Thomas Jefferson's lap.

Lewis and Clark were the first and most remarkable of a long string of American teams: Mutt and Jeff, Huck and Jim, Abbott and

Costello, Butch and Sundance, and the like. Add the young Shoshone woman Sacagawea—who was only in her home country and able to be something of a guide to the captains for a few days of a very long trip—and you have the essential elements of a national myth. Many people have since traced out where Lewis and Clark went—most recently and perhaps most readably Stephen Ambrose in *Undaunted Courage*.[2] Guides to the Lewis and Clark trail abound, and there are probably at least one hundred motels up and down the Missouri River named for Sacagawea, but very few have cared very much—except in the geographical sense—about exactly what Lewis and Clark said, and even fewer have paid attention to *how* they said it. Bernard DeVoto probably had some inkling that there was a rude literature in the *Journals*, but then did the worst thing you can to an epic, which is abridge it. Stephen Ambrose calls the *Journals* a "literary treasure" but is too busy with the history to elaborate.

To be fair, though, this important text has not been fully appreciated for what it is because of two centuries of incomplete and inadequate editing. All three editions previous to this excellent one from the University of Nebraska—Nicholas Biddle in 1814, Elliott Coues in 1892, and Reuben Gold Thwaites in 1904—were flawed by significant omission. The last raw journal material to turn up—sixty-seven pages of field notes in Clark's hand, with interpolations by Lewis—was not found until 1953, or published until 1962. But even if all the far-flung materials had been gathered and slotted together correctly, the unwieldy and rather forbidding format of the Coues and the Thwaites editions would have defeated most readers, and did defeat me several times. Thus my gratitude to the present editor, Gary Moulton, and his assistant editor, Thomas Dunlay, for bringing what I believe to be a national epic into plain view at last.

---

2. Simon and Schuster, 1996.

Captain Lewis and Captain Clark,[3] as many have noted, were unusually stable and levelheaded men; or at least they were while they were on this trip. As events came along, they dealt with them as calmly as possible. They knew that President Jefferson had sent them west not to write a narrative epic but to get the facts. They were told to measure everything and they measured everything that could be measured. It never occurred to either of them that they might produce a work of literature, but, by the force and immediacy of their expression, they accomplished the one essential thing that writers must do: they brought the reader along with them, up that meandering river and over those snowy peaks.

Besides the natural history, the geology, the weather, temperature, longitude, distances that they had to keep up with, they had also been enjoined by Jefferson to make friends with the Indians and find out as much as possible about the disposition of the various tribes along the way. This turned out to be trickier than the measuring. What they discovered right away about the Teton Sioux was that they were bullies. The captains made only one provisioning error: they neglected to bring enough of the ultra-desirable blue beads. The Sioux had already been spoiled by the many traders from the north; part of their bullying may have been strategic, a means of keeping open their vital trade link with the Mandans, from whom they got corn. Had the captains not managed to remain calm and firm—Clark only once drew his sword—the whole party might have been wiped out then and there in the fall of 1804.

From a literary standpoint, the main residue of these few tense days in September was William Clark's orthographical death-struggle with the word "Sioux," the moral equivalent of Beowulf's struggle with the sea monster. Clark's efforts to subdue this slippery word

---

3. Captain Clark, once Lewis's superior officer, was not technically a captain on this journey—the army stiffed him—but this awkward fact was concealed from the men.

were almost Joycean—unless I have miscounted he spelled it twenty-two different ways:

> Soues, Sous, Sisouex, Souex, Seouex, Sciox, Sciouexm, Sioux, Seaux, Sieux, Scouix, Seauex, Seauix, Souix, Siaux, Sious, Sceoux, Sieuex, Sceaux, Shoe, Soux, Souis

Of course anyone who has ever had any contact with an unmodernized text of the *Journals*—few enough—knows that Captain William Clark was one of the most defiant, as well as most inventive, spellers ever to attempt to use the English language. He may be said to have invented the concept of windchill when he described a forty-below Dakota day with the wind blowing as "Breizing." Despite his constant disregard for all orthographical rules Clark is never unclear; he is just exercising his right as an American to say things his own way.

Meriwether Lewis, who had for a time been Thomas Jefferson's secretary, was a far better speller and a meticulous reporter. The word "animal" did bother him—he usually spelled it with three a's—though he could describe the animals themselves with great precision. Captain Clark couldn't spell "animal," or "vegetable" either.

Because the captains frequently copied from each other's journals—sometimes part days, sometimes whole days—the effect as they proceed across the continent is that of a kind of lamination, an overlaying of two points of view and habits of expression.

Here for example are the two of them on the eventful day of May 14, 1805, when the Corps narrowly survived both a shipwreck and a grizzly bear. They were then on the upper Missouri, in present-day Montana. Lewis wrote:

> ...We had been halted by an occurrence, which now have to recappitulate, and which altho' happily passed without ruinous injury, I cannot recollect but with the utmost trepidation and

horror: this is the upseting and narrow escape of the white perogue It happened for us unfortunately this evening that Charbono [Toussaint Charbonneau, Sacagawea's husband] was at the helm of this Perogue, in stead of Drewyer [Drouillard], who had previously steered her; Charbono cannot swim and is perhaps the most timid waterman in the world; perhaps it was equally unluckey that Captain C. and myself were both on shore at that moment...; in this perogue were embarked, our papers, Instruments, books medicine, a great part of our merchandize and in short almost every article indispensably necessary to further the views, or insure the success of the enterprize in which we are now launched to the distance of 2200 miles. surfice it to say, that the Perogue was under sail when a sudon squawl of wind struck her obliquely, and turned her considerably, the steerman allarmed, in stead of putting her before the wind, lufted her up into it, the wind was so violent that it... instantly upset the perogue and would have turned her completely topsaturva, had it not been for the resistence mad by the oarning against the water;... Capt. C. and myself both fired our guns... but they did not hear us; such was their confusion and consternation at this moment, that they suffered the perogue to lye on her side for half a minute before they took the sail in, the perogue then wrighted but had filled within an inch of the gunwals; Charbono still crying to his god for mercy, had not yet recollected the rudder, nor could the repeated orders of the Bowsman, Cruzat [Cruzatte], bring him to his recollection untill he threatened to shoot him instantly if he did not take hold of the rudder and do his duty,... the fortitude resolution and good conduct of Cruzat saved her; he ordered 2 of the men to thow out the water with some kettles that fortunately were convenient.... I for a moment forgot my own situation, and involluntarily droped my gun, threw aside my shot pouch and was in the act of unbuttoning my coat, before I recollected the folly of the attempt I was about to make, which was to throw myself in the river and indevour to swim to the perogue; the perogue was three hundred yards distant, . . . the water so excessively could, and the stream rappid; had I undertaken this project therefore, there was a hundred to one but but what I should have paid the forfit of my life. . . . After having all matters arranged for the evening as well as the nature of the circumstances would permit, we thought it a proper occasion to console ourselves and cheer the sperits of our men and accordingly took a drink of grog and gave each man a gill of sperit.

To this Captain Clark adds only one detail:

. . . The articles which floated out was nearly all caught by the Squar [Sacagawea] who was in the rear. This accident had like to have cost us deerly. . . .

The grizzly bear, too, had like to have cost them dearly. Clark wrote:

Six good hunters of the party fired at a Brown or Yellow *Bear* Several times before they killed him, & indeed he had like to have defeated the whole party, he pursued them Seperately as they fired on him, and was near Catching Several of them one he pursued into the river, this bear was large & fat would way about 500 wt; I killed a Buffalow, & Capt. Lewis a Calf & a wolf this evening.

All in all, one feels that the Corps of Discovery deserved their gill of spirits at the conclusion of that eventful day, though a reprimand was surely in order for the crewman who allowed Toussaint Charbonneau to have any part in the handling of the vessel. A month before, on April 13, Charbonneau had made exactly the same mistake, causing a similar though not quite so dramatic panic. Indeed, as I read the *Journals* one of the comic subthemes of the narrative is the sublime incompetence of Toussaint Charbonneau, who did nothing much right his whole long life except stumble along beside the little Shoshone captive girl he had acquired from the Hidatsa and watch her become Sacagawea, myth-woman of the West.[4]

Many epic resemblances crop up in the Lewis and Clark narrative, for instance this little brush with the supernatural in South Dakota. Clark wrote:

> In a northerley direction from the mouth of this Creek in an imence Plain a high Hill is Situated, and appears of a Conic form and by the different nations of Indians in this quarter is Suppose to be the residence of Deavels. that they are in human form with remarkable large heads and about 18 Inches high, that they are Very watchfull and are arm'd with sharp arrows with which they Can Kill at a great distance; they are Said to Kill all persons who are So hardy as to attempt to approach the hill; they State that tradition informs them that many Indians have Suffered by these little people and among others three *Mahar* men fell a Sacrefise to their murceyless fury not many years Since....

The Corps of Discovery had its young Elpenor too—Elpenor being the young friend of Odysseus who got drunk at Circe's party, went to sleep on the roof, forgot he was on a roof, and stepped off and broke his neck. Lewis and Clark's young Elpenor was the likable Sergeant Charles Floyd, whose mistake was to dance too vigorously with the Omaha and Oto girls, after which he was "taken verry bad all at onc

---

4. In fairness, he *could* cook. Hired as an interpreter, Charbonneau was soon in demand for his signature dish, *boudin blanc*.

with the Beliose Chorlick." That was on August 18, 1804; by the 20th it was all over. Clark wrote:

> we Came to make a warm bath for Sergt. Floyd hopeing it would brace him a little, before we could get him into this bath he expired, with a great deel of composure, haveing Said to me before his death that he was going away and wished me to write a letter—we Buried him to the top of a high round hill over looking the river & Countrey for a great distance Situated just below a Small river without a name to which we name & call Floyds river, the Bluffs Sergts. Floyds Bluff—we buried him with all the honors of War and fixed a Ceeder post at his head with his name title & Day of the month and year Capt Lewis read the funeral Service over him after paying everry respect to the Body of this deceased man (who had at All times given us proofs of impatiality Sincurity to ourselves and good will to Serve his Countrey) we returned to the Boat & proceeded to the Mouth of the little river 30 yards wide & Camped a butifull evening....

Sergeant Charles Floyd was the only man lost by the Corps of Discovery on their trip of between seven and eight thousand miles through a wilderness, a remarkable tribute to the skills of the two captains—and also to their luck. Visitors to Sioux City, Iowa, today will find that Sergeant Floyd has not been forgotten; modern opinion is that he died of a ruptured appendix.

At times the reader wishes the narrative had a little more of the novel and a little less of the epic, mainly because of the vast range of characters the captains run into in this supposedly empty land. The scene at the Mandan villages in the winter of 1804–1805 was a veritable international soirée—if Dickens, Balzac, and Gogol could have been there, their pens would have been flying. The captains, though, were new boys on the block and had to step carefully; their job was to survive it, not describe it. Still, one would like to see more of Le Borgne (or the One-Eye), the domineering chief of the Hidatsa, whom even the present relatively nonjudgmental editors describe as brutal, ugly, lecherous, and homicidal—though dead loyal to his friends. Or René Jusseaume, whose name gave Captain Clark fits, a frontier hustler who had already been with the Mandans some fifteen years and was to last about another forty. The trader Alexander Henry the Younger described Jusseaume succinctly as "an old sneaking cheat," but it was Jusseaume who, when Sacagawea was in labor and her midwife Captain Lewis rather worried, suggested giving her two rings of a rattlesnake rattle. Captain Lewis, though skeptical, happened to have a rattlesnake rattle handy, two rings of which were given to Sacagawea in water. In only a few minutes her son Jean Baptiste Charbonneau (Little Pomp to Captain Clark, who loved him dearly) was among the living.

Little Pomp and his parents went all the way to the Pacific with the Corps of Discovery, and the baby's mere presence was an immense help to the captains in their relations with the Indians, who reckoned correctly that a war party would not be traveling with a woman and a baby. Captain Clark offered to educate Little Pomp, and the Charbonneaus, good parents, in due course delivered him to St. Louis. William Clark took the young boy into his own home; later, then a youth, Baptiste attracted the attention of Prince Paul of Wurttemberg, who took him to Europe and educated him in his castle near Stuttgart. When Baptiste Charbonneau came back to America he spoke four languages and became a reliable and much sought-after guide.

As Captain Lewis first discerned with joy the dim outlines of the Rocky Mountains, we can, in the spacious flow of this narrative, discern the dim outlines of many genres to come: the domestic sitcom, for example. In the saga of the Charbonneaus—Toussaint the bumbling husband, Sacagawea the competent wife calmly picking up the articles that had floated out of the boat—you have the axle of

American television comedies from *The Honeymooners* to *Malcolm in the Middle*.

Though a bumbler and "a man of no particular merit" (Lewis), Toussaint Charbonneau outlived them all, Sacagawea, the captains, Le Borgne, plus several members of the Corps who were quite a bit more competent: George Drouillard and John Colter for two. Once William Clark became superintendent of Indian affairs, Charbonneau got back on the payroll and stayed on it. He may even have squeezed into a group picture, Karl Bodmer's *The Travelers Meeting With Minataree Indians Near Fort Clark*, in which a figure in buckskins who is possibly Charbonneau is seen interpreting for Bodmer's patron, Prince Maximilian of Wied-Neuwied. This is pretty good for a man who twice within the space of a month narrowly missed drowning himself, his wife, his baby, and several companions in the Missouri River some thirty years before.

But that's looking ahead. As the trek goes on, the West comes to seem less a place of wild savagery than a place of wild zaniness. The Corps splits up, and the lack of mailboxes is severely felt. Captain Lewis leaves Captain Clark a note on a pole, but a beaver chews down the pole and swims off with the note. Over the mountains at last but apprehensive of slim provisions downriver, the captains purchase forty dogs, a barking larder. Then there's the problem of anticlimax, felt by so many vacationers since. The getting there is rarely as good as the going. "Ocian in view! O! the joy!" (Clark) But it wasn't the ocean, it was only the estuary, and soon they were stuck on the north side of the Columbia River, where it was very wet. "O! how horriable is the day." (Clark) The collective mood is not improved by watching the Chinooks zip through towering waves in their canoes as if on a freeway. The Corps had no such skills. The captains discouraged moping, but some moped anyway, while others slogged through the drizzle and kept busy by getting venereal diseases from local lasses who had previously been visited by sailors from big boats.

But spring comes, the snows melt in the passes, and the Corps heads home. In Montana, near the Marias River, while traveling with some Piegans (Blackfeet), there is an unfortunate scuffle over a rifle one of the Field brothers has carelessly left unguarded. Reuben Field comes to his brother's assistance and stabs the would-be thief to death. Captain Lewis wounds another, who shoots back and then crawls off into some rocks. This occurred on July 27, 1806. If Joe Field had just been more careful with his gun the Corps would have made it across the West and back without hurting anyone. A few days later, while hunting, the usually reliable Pierre Cruzatte, the Frenchman who saved the pirogue, mistook Captain Lewis for an elk and shot him in the thigh, a painful wound.

Back in the Mandan villages by August of 1806, they pay off Toussaint Charbonneau, who was due $500.33⅓ cents precisely. Clark wrote:

> We also took our leave of T. Chabono, his Snake Indian wife and their Son Child who had accompanied us on our rout to the pacific Ocean in the Capacity of interpreter and interpretes. . . . I offered to take their little Son a butifull promising Child who is 19 months old to which they both himself & wife wer willing provided the Child had been weaned.

But the child hasn't been weaned and the couple is left to look for another job, Sacagawea no doubt aware that without the captains to restrain him and yell at him Toussaint will soon be smacking her again. Out of the mists she came, back into the mists she goes. The captains make the One-Eye a present of their swivel gun but the chief still can't be bothered to go to Washington with them and meet the Great Father. It is on to St. Louis and, perhaps, another anticlimax. Clark writes: "a fine morning we commenced wrighting &c."

There had been, however, transcendent moments, such as this one, August 12, 1805 (Lewis):

> At the distance of 4 miles further the road took us to the most distant fountain of the waters of the mighty Missouri in surch of which we had spent so many toilsome days and wristless nights. thus far I had accomplished one of those great objects on which my mind had been unalterably fixed for many years, judge then of the pleasure I felt in allaying my thirst with this pure and ice cold water. ... two miles below McNeal had exultantly stood with a foot on each side of this little rivulet and thanked his god that he had lived to bestride the mighty & heretofore deemed endless Missouri....

Like many teammates, once the great game was over the captains separated. Exactly when and how they produced this onflowing 200,000-word narrative is complicated; the present editors lay out these complications intelligently and fully. Captain Clark went on to a long and active career, most of it spent as superintendent of Indian affairs, which allowed him to hire the Charbonneaus again. Three years after the trip ended, Meriwether Lewis killed himself in a roadhouse on the Natchez Trace. He succumbed, perhaps, to that melancholy which Thomas Jefferson had noted in him long before, and which, perhaps, had been held in check by the demands of a great endeavor.

Lewis and Clark, two eighteenth-century soldiers writing the robust language of Johnson and Fielding—so robust that their first editor, Nicholas Biddle, felt obliged to put some of it in Latin—were immediately and justly applauded for what they did, but, to my knowledge, they have never been adequately applauded for what they wrote. For almost two hundred years their strong words waited, there but not there, printed but not read: our silent epic. But words *can* wait: now the captains' writings have at last spilled out, and fully, in this regal edition, which also includes the journals or narratives of four other members of the Corps of Discovery: John Ordway, Joseph Whitehouse, Patrick Gass, and Charles Floyd. It will be good if some day there can be a cheaper, popular edition, but not, I hope, an abridged one. Keep it all! Even the measurements, which are part of the achievement too. If we are lucky enough to have an epic, we should play by the epic's rules.

Chapter 11

SACAGAWEA'S NICKNAME

Many millions of Native American women have lived and died on the North American continent, and yet, until quite recently, only two—Pocahantas and Sacagawea—have left even faint tracings of their personalities on history; and, in both cases, these delicate, shadowy outlines have long since been heavily marked over by the crude pencil of legend. Students of either woman have to carefully peel legend from fact, and to discard much overstatement. If this is done with tact and care it is just possible to get, now and then, a few glimpses of the women who once were.

I am not a student of Pocahantas but I might mention one or two parallels between her life and Sacagawea's: both married older white men, both bore sons, both traveled far from their people, and both died in their twenties. Pocahantas converted to Christianity, got in a big ship, went to England, met James I, died in 1617 (a year after Shakespeare), and is buried at Gravesend.

Sacagawea, traveling in a much smaller boat with her husband and her baby, journeyed west with Lewis and Clark and the Corps of Discovery; she saw, at her insistence, the Pacific Ocean, and what was left of a whale. On the return trip in 1806, traveling on the Missouri River, she was put ashore with her husband, the expedition's chief interpreter, Toussaint Charbonneau, and their son, Jean Baptiste, at the Mandan villages in present-day North Dakota, where the Corps had picked them up the year before. Three years later she sent her son to be educated by William Clark. The best evidence suggests that she died at the fort of the fur mogul Manuel Lisa, in South Dakota, of a "putrid fever," in 1812. The trader John Luttig, who promptly reported her death to Captain Clark, called her "a good and the best woman in the Fort."

According to their journals, Lewis and Clark met Sacagawea late in 1804, while she was pregnant with her son, whom Captain Lewis helped deliver; they dropped the Charbonneaus off in August of 1806, which means that Sacagawea was visible to the eye of history for something less than two years. What does history see?

First, it sees that for a young woman to travel across the upper West at the beginning of the nineteenth century with thirty-two men and a baby was no bed of roses. Her nautically challenged husband twice nearly dumped her and the baby accidentally into the icy Missouri River. Because of her infant she and her husband slept in the captain's tent, a proximity that may not always have been easy. In June of 1805 she got seriously ill—Captain Lewis, who carefully nursed her back to health, suspected some blockage of the menses: she suffered all this while managing a young child and a cranky husband.

Legend has it that Sacagawea was a guide, but this legend is an early-twentieth-century fabrication. She was brought along because she could speak Shoshone; her guiding consisted mainly of identifying Beaverhead Rock, in southwestern Montana, a landmark the captains could probably have figured out for themselves. Luckily the Corps did stumble onto the very band of Snake Indians Sacagawea had been kidnapped from; there's a moment of happy emotion when she runs into one of the young women who had been abducted with her. There's also a bit of uplift when it turns out that her own brother, Cameahwait, is the leader of this band; and yet there are always likely to be problems with going home, as Thomas Wolfe was later to declare. The husband Sacagawea had been married to before her abduction had two other wives and didn't want her. Women enjoyed very little status with the Shoshone, as the Captains Lewis and Clark tirelessly point out. Cameahwait, Sacagawea's brother, was hardly overflowing with family feeling—when it came to selling horses to the whites he drove a hard and at times tenuous bargain.

During the seven months that it takes the Corps to get up the Missouri River, over the Rocky Mountains, and down the Columbia River, both Captain Lewis and Captain Clark struggle somewhat awkwardly with what to call Sacagawea. For long stretches, in their *Journals*, she is simply "the Indian woman," or "Charbono's Snake Indian wife," or, more rarely, "the Squar." There is a certain uneasiness in these references, though. After all, this young woman slept with her husband in their tent; they saw her every day, as she does her best to be helpful, digging up Jerusalem artichokes, gathering fennel, chopping elk bones and boiling out a fine grease. Reluctantly, and never very successfully, they begin to call her Sacagawea, which they spell several different ways. By this time both men have considerable respect for Sacagawea, and Captain Clark really likes her, as will be seen.

Finally they—or is it "they"?—decide on a nickname, Janey: but here's the catch! The nickname is only mentioned once in the 5,448 pages of the University of Nebraska edition of the *Journals*.[1] It is used again, by Captain Clark, in the expeditionary correspondence.

The occasion on which the nickname is revealed—again, by Captain Clark—is itself of some interest. Mired in misery on the north bank of the Columbia, drenched almost every day, the captains decided to take a vote on where to construct a winter camp. All the men voted, including York, Captain Clark's black servant; and Janey voted, too, indicating that she would prefer to camp where there were lots of potatoes. This sudden granting of suffrage-in-the-wilderness

1. In Volume 6.

strikes me as pretty amazing, as does the offhand revelation of the nickname. Was the nickname in general use, or was it just Captain Clark's pet name for a young woman he had come to like? The three members of the Corps who left supplementary narratives and who knew Sacagawea—John Ordway, Joseph Whitehouse, and Patrick Gass—mainly just call her "the interpreter's wife," in Gass's case, "our squaw."

Be that as it may, Janey voted on the location of the camp, and that was not her only act of self-assertion. In January 1806, reports reached them of a beached whale. Captain Clark decided to take a party to the beach and attempt to secure some whale oil, at which point the fat—or, in this case, the blubber—hit the fire. Clark writes:

> The last evening Shabono and his Indian woman was very impatient to be permitted to go with me, and was therefore indulged. She observed that She had traveled a long way with us to See the great waters, and now that that monstrous fish was also to be Seen, She thought it verry hard that She could not be permitted to See either (She had never yet been to the Ocian.)

After all she had put up with, Janey was determined to see the sights, and did not even have to throw much of a fit to get her way. Not only did she initiate suffrage in the far West, she initiated tourism, even feminism, as well.

That solitary, haunting "Janey" does make a reader wonder. As any student of the *Journals* will soon discover, William Clark served as Thomas Jefferson's fashion eye, delivering copious reports on the dress of the various tribes the party met. In some cases the skimpier the female costumes, the more copious Clark's notes become. Here, for example, is the conclusion of his long description of the bark petticoats worn by the Wahkaikum women:

> ...The Same materials which Serves as well for a girdle as to hold in place the Strans of bark which forms the tissue, and which Strans, Confined in the middle, hang with their ends pendulous from the waiste, the whole being of Suffcent thickness when the female Stands erect to conceal those parts useally covered from famaliar view, but when she stoops of places herself in any other attitudes this battery of Venus is not altogether impervious to the penetrating eye of the amorite...

This is not the only time the battery of Venus comes in for mention in the *Journals*—quite a few of those wild western women seemed to run around half undressed.

Both captains seem to have stood clear of native women, though Nez Percé legend does claim that William Clark fathered a son by the sister of their great chief Red Grizzly. Whatever the truth of that, it is plain that William Clark had little of the Puritan in him. He was not supposed to touch, but he could look, and he did look.

As for his relations with Janey, I wouldn't suggest a romance or even a flirtation, but I do think the two had a friendly rapport, part of their bond being Captain Clark's deep fondness for her little boy. Mothers will frequently soften a little toward a man who really likes their child, and Captain Clark just couldn't get enough of Little Pomp.

I believe Sacagawea came to like this man; she showed it by now and then giving him little gifts. Once some bread she had been saving for her son got soaked, so she gave it, instead, to Captain Clark, who ate it gratefully. On another occasion, Sacagawea gave him a nice basket and two dozen weasel tails. It seems unlikely that she would have saved up weasel tails for any other member of the Corps.

How Sacagawea was treated by other members of the company, and what she thought of them, is not easy to discern. With Captain Lewis, who nursed both herself and her son through dangerous illnesses, she seems to have remained businesslike. Lewis, for his part, is mostly neutral about Sacagawea, though he does condescend a bit now and then, suggesting at one point that it would take only a few trinkets to make her happy. It is a pity he didn't sketch her. He drew an excellent fish, and the head of a gull, but left no image of the woman he traveled with for thousands of miles.

My belief that there was a bit of an attachment between Sacagawea and William Clark is bolstered by a remarkable letter that Clark addressed to Toussaint Charbonneau only three days after the Corps dropped the little family off at the Mandan villages, leaving them to struggle on as best they could.

The letter is addressed "On board the Pirogue, Near the Ricara Village, Aug 20 1806." Clark first expresses his worry: "Your present situation with the Indians gives me some concern. . . ." The captain then proceeds to offer Charbonneau the moon if he will bring Sacagawea and their child on down to St. Louis. He offers to furnish him a piece of land, and horses, cattle, hogs. He offers to help him secure an inventory of trade goods if he wants to become a trader. Of Sacagawea he says this:

> your woman who accompanied us on that long dangerous and fatigueing rout to the Pacific Ocean and back deserved a greater reward for her attentions and services on that rout than we had it in our power to give her at the Mandans. . . .

He then repeats his offer to take "my danceing little Baptiest" and raise him as his own child, urging that if Charbonneau does "bring down your son famm[ily] Janey had best come along with you to take care of the boy until I get him. . . ."

It seems that Charbonneau at least knew of the nickname; it was Charbonneau himself who had chosen to get off at the Mandan villages, a busy trade center where an interpreter stood a good chance of making a living.

William Clark was undoubtedly sincere in his concern for Charbonneau's family. He did educate his "danceing little Baptiest," and he helped Toussaint Charbonneau many times and continued to help him long after Sacagawea was dead.

Still, that letter, written in a boat off the Arikara village, shows us something more than just a military man who suddenly realizes he has not sufficiently rewarded a subordinate; it shows us a family man who suddenly misses his family, for Sacagawea's family, for many long and strenuous months, had been William Clark's family. He missed that little boy, and he missed Janey.

Many years later, in listing the dead of the expedition in his cash book and journal for 1825–1828, William Clark essayed that tricky name one last time:

Sar car Ja we a   Dead

How delighted he would have been if he could have known that Janey's difficult name would live as long as his.

Chapter 12

OLD MISERY

1.

The Missouri River has been much used but not much loved. An argument could be made that, historically, it is the most important waterway in North America, but significance does not always breed affection. People love domesticated rivers—the Seine, the Thames, the Danube—or even semi-domesticated rivers—the Nile, the Mississippi. They don't love the Missouri, although they may fear it.

Some of the rivermen who have to work with the Missouri day in and day out call it Old Misery, because of the difficulty of getting a boat up it or down it. Its snags are so legendary that the painter George Catlin, in a mot of which he was proud, called it the River of Sticks (Styx), and this despite the fact that he himself went up in some luxury on the steamboat *Yellowstone* on that vessel's maiden voyage in 1832. Catlin also called the Missouri a "filthy abyss," "a hell of waters," "a huge deformity of water," and so forth. But for the fact that he refused to illustrate the pioneer ethnologist Henry Schoolcraft's extensive researches into Native American life, thus making a powerful enemy, Catlin would probably have succeeded in selling his laboriously accumulated Indian portfolio to the nation. The portfolio consisted of 310 portraits and 200 other pictures, representing 48 tribes. When the sale fell through—narrowly defeated in the Congress—

Catlin left America, showed his pictures in London and Paris, and lived as a kind of mountebank, traveling as far as Tierra del Fuego. Schoolcroft did give him a nice blurb when his book came out.

His fellow artist, the Haitian-born, mostly French John James Audubon, who went up the Missouri in 1843, didn't bother bad-mouthing the river, preferring to bad-mouth Catlin instead:

> We have seen much handsome scenery but nothing at all comparing with Catlin's descriptions; his book must, after all, be altogether a humbug. . . .

The most common complaints against the river were snags—trees, stumps, branches—and mud. Captain William Clark estimated that every pint of the Missouri's water would yield a wineglass of ooze—or mud. Catlin claimed that if he dropped a white shell in a glass of Missouri water he could only detect the shell from a distance of an eighth of inch.

Mark Twain didn't write much about the Missouri—he had given his heart to the Mississippi, but the paragraph he does devote to it, at the beginning of *Roughing It*, has his usual snap:

> We were six days going from St. Louis to "St. Jo"—a trip that was so dull, sleepy, eventless that it left no more impression on my memory that if the duration had been six minutes instead of that many days. No record is left in my mind now, concerning it, but a confused jumble of savage looking snags, which we deliberately walked over with one wheel or the other; and of reefs which we butted and butted, and then retired from and climbed over in some softer place; and of sandbars which we roosted on occasionally, and rested, and then got out our crutches and spanned over. In fact, the boat might almost have gone to St. Jo by land, for she was walking most of the time

> anyway... the Captain said she was a "bully boat" and all she wanted was a bigger wheel. I thought she wanted a pair of stilts, but had the deep sagacity not to say so....

These few complaints can stand for thousands. The Missouri was a voracious river, draining more than half a million square miles of canyon and plain. It constantly ate its own banks, trees and all, so many trees that the editor Timothy Flint said that in places the river resembled a field of dead trees—indeed, the Swiss artist Karl Bodmer painted just such a scene in the great series of watercolors he did in 1833–1834 for his patron Prince Maximilian of Wied-Neuwied.

Nonetheless, for a century and a half, the Missouri functioned as a kind of superhighway. It was the best road to the deep West, traveled by everybody who was anybody—painters, princes, generals, capitalists, mountain men, adventurers of several nations—as well as the merely hopeful, the many thousands of nameless immigrants who were just looking for a little piece of land, a parcel of America, to call their own; these hopefuls were willing to risk any danger and endure any hardship to secure their little homeplace.

2.

The sight of moving water is affecting—humans love to walk by it, build beside it, fish in it, bathe in it, or merely stand on a bridge and look at it. Even though unstable itself, the sight of moving water makes people feel somehow more stable. City dwellers come to feel that they own the rivers running through their cities, even while recognizing that nobody really owns rivers. Some of the greatest buildings in Europe can be seen from riverboats on the Thames or the Seine, the Danube or the Rhine. New York can be seen from the Hudson and the East River, Washington from the Potomac, Pittsburgh from the Ohio, and so on. Even a few small cities still have vital waterfronts: Louisville, Memphis, Baton Rouge.

But there are rivers long and wild, with no great buildings or notable cities beside them: the Lena and the Yenesei, the Congo, the Yangtze, even the Amazon (despite that opera house in Manaus).

The Missouri is a river of the second sort. When low and sluggish it invites contempt, when in flood a kind of horror. Here, for example, is the first recorded European impression—at least the first that we know of for sure. Father Jacques Marquette and his companion Jolliet were drifting down the Mississippi, gazing at some "ruined castles" said to be the home of Indian gods, "when they were suddenly aroused by a real danger."

> A torrent of yellow mud rushed furiously athwart the calm blue current of the Mississippi: boiling and surging and sweeping in its course logs, branches, uprooted trees. They had reached the mouth of the Missouri, where that savage river, descending from its career through a vast unknown of barbarism, poured its turbid floods onto the bosom of its gentler sister. The light canoes whirled on the vortex like dry leaves in an angry brook. "I never," writes Marquette, "saw anything more terrific"; but they escaped with their fright, and held their way down the turbulent and swollen current of a now united river. They passed the lonely forests that covered the destined city of St. Louis, and, a few days later, saw on their left the mouth of the stream to which the Iroquois had given the well merited name of the beautiful river. . . .

Thus the historian Francis Parkman, reporting for Marquette and editorializing as he does. The Missouri is "yellow," a baleful color to begin with. It "careers through a vast unknown of barbarism"; it compares unfavorably with the Ohio, the beautiful river that comes from the east—that is, from civilization, the opposite of barbarism, though many of the Iroquois' captives would have allowed that they were barbaric enough; but Francis Parkman did like to dramatize his histories; he picks up "turbid," one of George Catlin's favorite adjectives. Catlin, like Parkman, after all had books to sell. A factor in his failure to sell his portfolio to the nation was the fear among some congressmen that showing so many Indians in their splendor—and their humanity—might arouse undue sympathy in the public at large, making it that much harder to displace the soon-to-be-evicted Five Civilized Tribes and get them started on their woeful journey along the Trail of Tears. In the end many of the pictures did end up in the Smithsonian, donated by the widow of one of Catlin's creditors.

For all his crankiness, George Catlin was no fool. He saw quite clearly that the native life he was recording would soon vanish; the very fact that he could travel all the way to the Yellowstone River on a steamboat told him that. The trickiest part of his task was convincing the Indians that, by taking their image, he was not stealing part of themselves. The photographers who would soon flood the West had the same problem. Catlin quickly learned that the chiefs who posed for him would not tolerate any attempt to draw them in profile—where was the other half of them? The subjects (and the medicine men) wanted to know.

The sale of his portfolio to the nation failed, but before he departed these shores (for thirty-one years) George Catlin took the trouble to invent the Wild West show, a species of which he produced in 1839.

3.

The American West as we know it today came about in response to European—particularly Spanish—disappointment. Nothing that any European power ever did in the Americas prior to our own century equaled, for drama, what Spain did in its initial strikes at Mexico and Peru. Between 1519, when Cortez took Tenochtitlan (Mexico City) and 1533, when Atahuallpa, the Inca, was strangled in Peru, two old, elaborate empires collapsed before the aggression of a handful of European invaders. The treasures these two countries yielded were not be easily matched. Though of course, in the long term, the Spanish took plenty out of North America.

The British and French came a little late to the New World party. Having found no Mexico and no Peru they were not troubled by the sense of letdown that the Spanish felt. In the western regions, when they finally got there, both furs and souls interested the French—for the British, furs alone were enough. Even though the English ultimately won the struggle for Canada, the French didn't really leave, and still haven't. Spend a night in Quebec, or Montreal.

The Hudson's Bay Company, the Microsoft of its era, could not have flourished as it did without legions of French trappers. Lewis and Clark themselves had a number of French *engagés* when they started up the river in 1804. By my reckoning there were some forty small expeditions up the Missouri River before Lewis and Clark, many of which depended on the expertise, and the muscle, of French boatmen; and St. Louis, the Gateway, was at first a French city.

It seems clear now that the United States at the end of the eighteenth century was poised to make an irresistible surge to the west, but this surge was much assisted by French calculation—specifically, Napoleon's calculation, seconded by his minister, Talleyrand, not to compete. The latter had not enjoyed his exile in America, though it probably enabled him to keep his head. Napoleon hadn't enjoyed his defeats in Santo Domingo, either. Perhaps both men recognized that their genius was continental. Napoleon had England, Austria, and Spain to think about, with Russia already in his dreams. The American West was both too empty and too far.

The other great player in the story of the Missouri River, Thomas Jefferson, thus received an extraordinary plum, the Louisiana Purchase, the deal for which "closed," as the realtors say, just before Lewis and

Clark started up the river in 1804. Jefferson's principal worry had been that the British would somehow manage to seal us off at the Mississippi. He worried less about Spain, perhaps reckoning that thousands of little American mice would slowly nibble away until the Spanish empire in the West had been quietly consumed.

Since the 1780s at least, Thomas Jefferson had been looking for someone to ascend the Missouri River and make a thorough report; the first person he approached was George Rogers Clark, William Clark's big brother. George Rogers Clark declined. Then Jefferson tried Joseph Ledyard, a wanderer, who decided that the smart approach would be to sprint across Siberia and do America west to east. The Russians, however, promptly kicked Ledyard out, leaving Jefferson to try and tempt, separately, two botanists, Moses Marshall and André Michaux. Marshall declined and Michaux turned out to be a schemer whose schemes did not include the Missouri River.

The achievement of Lewis and Clark has rightly dominated American thinking about the early West. Most Americans who think historically at all probably recall that there were some French trappers paddling their canoes around somewhere in the northern reaches of the Missouri's drainage system; they may also recall that there were some Spaniards over in Santa Fe, where all the nice New York shops now have branches. A few may even remember that there was once something called the Fur Trade, but that's about as far as historical reflection gets, in regard to the West.

For those who want to look deeper, two excellent books should be mentioned: A. P. Nasatir's *Before Lewis and Clark*,[1] and Louise Barry's *The Beginnings of the West*.[2] These books contain accurate and formidable lists of the travelers—dozens of them, most of them

---

1. Two volumes, St. Louis Historical Documents Foundation, 1952; University of Nebraska Press, 1990.

2. Kansas State Historical Society, 1972.

Spanish and French—who were out and about in the West well before Lewis and Clark. Such lists are useful mainly because it shows how very determined the European powers were to find whatever was valuable in the West and secure as much of the valuables as possible for themselves or their crowns.

The reader might wonder why I mention the Spanish explorers in a piece about the Missouri River, since few of them ranged that far east or northwest. I put them in because the Spanish were extremely vigorous in their efforts to extend their trading reach. When Lewis and Clark finally got to Idaho and began to purchase horses from the local tribes, they discovered that some of the horses bore Spanish brands. The Spanish authorities in New Mexico were fully aware of what Lewis and Clark meant for the future of their territory. They sent four expeditions to try to head them off, three under Pedro Vial and one under Facundo Malgres; the latter captured Zebulon Pike two years later. But the captains slipped by.

Besides, from the mid-eighteenth to the mid-nineteenth centuries the great trade portal in the interior West was Santa Fe—Spanish until 1821, then Mexican. There was then no settlement in the upper West to compare with it. Santa Fe provided the logical, and for long the dominant, trade link with St. Louis, and a great many of the well-known soldiers of fortune who went up the Missouri did so only as far as the overland embarkation points in northern Missouri or Kansas: St. Joseph, Independence, Westport Landing. The Missouri took an almost continuous stream of traders north to the jumping off points. From whence they jumped off and headed West, for Santa Fe.

4.

On their way back down the Missouri in the summer of 1806, Lewis and Clark amiably discharged the expedition member John Colter, so that he could go trapping with two adventurous souls Captain Clark had run into on the Yellowstone. These bold trappers were Joseph Dixon and Forrest Hancock, and John Colter's decision to join them on the dangerous Yellowstone might be said to have ushered in the era of the Mountain Men, a colorful and various company that eventually grew to include Kit Carson, Jim Bridger, Jedediah Smith, Hugh Glass, Thomas Fitzpatrick, James Beckwourth, Charles Bent, Old Bill Williams, Peg-Leg Smith, Uncle Dick Wotton, Ezekiel Williams, Zenas Leonard, James Pattie, and many more. Though the greatest of the these was probably Jedediah Smith, one of the few mountain men who sought geographical knowledge for its own sake, and added much to what was then known about the interior West, the only names from that roster that might register with the public now today are Kit Carson and Jim Bridger, and few could describe with accuracy what either of those men did.

What all mountain men did, first and foremost, was to attempt to catch and skin as many as possible of the millions of small fur-bearing animals that inhabited the prairie or mountain streams, an activity that very often brought them into sharp and sometimes fatal conflict with native tribes. It says something about the fierce force of commercial instinct that so much effort could be expended, and such great distances crossed, to establish trade relations with scattered bands of Indians whose groups were small in number and usually very poor. And yet the dependence of even the poorest tribes on the white man's hatchets and fish hooks was established almost immediately, pelts being what the whites got in return. Once a trading relationship was established, the Indians fought hard to maintain their advantage.

In this regard the river Indians along the Missouri, particularly the Arikara and the Mandans, enjoyed a distinct advantage. The great river made them reachable, and allowed them, very quickly, to establish themselves as middle men between the white traders and nomadic tribes such as the Sioux. The failure of even well-armed fur traders to crack this hegemony drove the mountain men, for a time, off the river and into the mountains from whence their dangerous profession took its name.

The climax of this short chapter in the history of American commerce came in 1823, when the Arikara defeated a company of trappers led by the flamboyant but not always sufficiently cautious William Ashley. The Arikara won that fight decisively; and a foolish attempt to punish them by militia commanded by Colonel Henry Leavenworth—after whom a famous federal prison is named—ended in fiasco as well. The Arikara and the Mandans continued to hold the central section of the Missouri for a time, though not for long. Smallpox, a weapon deadlier than cannon, decimated the river villages in the 1830s—by the end of that bitter decade the Arikara and the Mandans had been reduced almost to remnant populations.

William Ashley, not daunted, then helped to develop the rendezvous system, in which all the mountain men in the central Rockies would gather in a certain spot once a season to trade their furs, swap stores, and in general enjoy a great binge. (A quaint vestige of these wild gatherings is the annual rally of Harley-Davidson riders that have recently been assembling in Sturgis, South Dakota.)

Almost all the mountain men mentioned in my list used the Missouri River at one time or another in their careers; their contribution to the lore and legend of the Missouri has been vast but their direct contribution to its literature is minute. A few of them left short journals (Jedediah Smith) or dictated autobiographies (Kit Carson). Others with the aid of obedient ghostwriters, spun long, self-glorifying narratives (Beckwourth). Almost all of these men now have biographies, sometimes several biographies, but these mostly had to wait until the middle of the twentieth century, and vary greatly in quality.

Few of these mountain men would have bothered to complain about the Missouri River and its whims—complaint was left to the aesthetes who soon came. The mountain men, following Lewis and Clark's lead, took a matter-of-fact approach to the river. A mountain man, noticing an acre or so of the riverbank about to fall into the water, would bestir himself so as not to be underneath it; but he would not allow such trifles to disturb his sleep.

From the return of Lewis and Clark in 1806 to the close of the Indian wars in the 1880s the Missouri remained the superhighway, its function as a quick road to the deep West not yet usurped by the railroads—although the railroads were rapidly closing in. The Union Pacific and the Northern Pacific soon divided the carrier functions that had once belonged almost solely to Old Misery.

5.

For the Indians of the central Missouri the 1830s were the decade of smallpox, a scourge that destroyed forever their power as river-keepers.

For artists, though, the 1830s provided a golden moment, the last moment in fact when it was possible to capture in oil or watercolor or charcoal sketch the great diversity of the native peoples of the West at the height of their splendor and strength. Three artists in particular profited from this moment: George Catlin, who worked for himself, Karl Bodmer, who worked for Prince Maximilian of Wied-Neuwied, and Alfred Jacob Miller, who was taken on by the great Scottish sportsman William Drummond Stewart. Jean Baptiste Charbonneau, Sacagawea's son, also worked for a time for the flamboyant Scot, helping to gather animals for his game park back in Scotland.

These three painters shared a collective bonanza: they got to the right places at the right times. Alfred Jacob Miller went west along the Platte and into the Rockies. Catlin and Bodmer both stuck to the river; each spent time at Fort Union, at the Missouri's junction with the Yellowstone, and Bodmer went on, with his persistent prince, all the way to Fort Mackenzie, which was about as far as boats went on the Missouri in that day.

Catlin, as I have said, went upriver in 1832, Bodmer in 1833–1834, and Miller in 1837. By the time their Indian pictures were shown many of their sitters were already dead of smallpox. Ironically, Catlin's Indian gallery was touring Europe just as Karl Bodmer was putting the final, exacting touches on his wonderful, delicate aquatints. Although neither Bodmer nor his prince liked Catlin's work, both hoped that some of his popularity would rub off and yield a few subscriptions for Bodmer's expensive albums. Catlin's small fame didn't rub off, but Bodmer's work survived. His extraordinary watercolor *Mih-tuha-gang-kush*, which shows a Mandan village on the Missouri's freezing banks—it was 46 below the day Bodmer made the sketch—remains, for me at least, the summit of Missouri River art. Nothing has ever caught so well the bleakness of those hills and that river in winter's heart.

Karl Bodmer must have felt that he never wanted to be in a place that exposed or that cold again; he spent the rest of his life drawing cozy forest scenes for French magazines. Yet his and his prince's great work, *Reise in das Innere Amerika in die Jahren 1832 bis 1834*—though commercially a failure of such proportions that only a prince could have afforded it—remains probably the greatest treasure among artworks dealing with the American West.

6.

When I began this essay I thought I would follow Missouri River narratives from Father Marquette in the seventeenth century to Custer and Cody, near the end of the nineteenth. If there were forty or fifty expeditions that followed the river for at least some little distance before Lewis and Clark, hundreds poured up the river in the decades after the captains came home. Many of these travelers left at least some scraps of narrative: Bradbury and Brackenridge, Prince Maximilian and Prince Paul, Zebulon Pike, Stephen Long, John Frémont, and the various surveyors; Washington Irving and Timothy Flint; Sherman, Sheridan, Miles, the Custers, Crook; a medley of Indian chiefs, including Red Cloud and Sitting Bull; bureaucrats and scientists by the score; Ned Buntline, Wild Bill Hickok, Calamity Jane, and, as I have said, virtually all the mountain men.

I thought it might be fun to ramble around in all those purple autobiographies and pull out a quote here and a quote there: but that was before I read *The Journals of the Lewis and Clark Expedition* in the thirteen-volume University of Nebraska edition, wonderfully and wisely edited by Gary E. Moulton, after which reading the purple autobiographies ceased to be half as much fun. Lewis and Clark loom over the narrative literature of the West as the Rockies loom over the rivers that run through them. These *Journals* are to the narrative of the American West as the *Iliad* is to the epic or as *Don Quixote* is to the novel: a first exemplar so great as to contain in embryo the genre's full potential. The narrative writing about the West that came before Lewis and Clark seems fragmentary and slight; what came after them seems insipid and slight, lacking both the scale and the force of those *Journals*.

By executing their mission so ably, and by describing it so fully, Lewis and Clark claimed the West for America—and the claim succeeded. That their words, in the unabridged Nebraska version, followed their deeds by nearly two hundred years doesn't matter very much. We now know the deeds in fine detail. But the happy year that I spent with these *Journals* cost me my appetite for the musings of Libbie Custer or the exaggerations of Buffalo Bill Cody.

The only supplements that really add anything to what Lewis and Clark left us are the albums of the three painters: Catlin, Bodmer, Miller—with Audubon's *Quadrupeds* as a welcome fourth. Very fortunately the painters followed closely enough upon the captains to be able to record the native people's great vigor before disease and conflict destroyed it. Thanks to the character, courage, and ability of these few men we can now know what the West was like before the prairie was plowed, the buffalo killed, the native peoples broken, and the mighty Missouri damned.